Quickclose™ is a registered trademark of Grant Cardone © 2009.
Information-Assisted Selling™ is a registered trademark of Grant Cardone © 1998.

Published by John Wiley & Sons, Inc., Hoboken, New Jersey.

Published simultaneously in Canada.

For general information on our other products and services or for technical support, please contact our Customer Care Department within the United States at (800) 762-2974, outside the United States at (317) 572-3993 or fax (317) 572-4002.

Wiley also publishes its books in a variety of electronic formats. Some content that appears in print may not be available in electronic books. For more information about Wiley products, visit our web site at www.wiley.com.

Library of Congress Cataloging-in-Publication Data:

Cardone, Grant.
  If you're not first, you're last : sales strategies to dominate your market and beat your competition / Grant Cardone.
    p. cm.
  ISBN 978-0-470-62435-7 (cloth)
  1. Success in business. 2. Strategic planning. 3. Organizational learning.
  I. Title. II. Title: If you are not first, you are last.
  HF5386.C254 2010
  658.8'2—dc22   2010004480

Printed in the United States of America

13 12

Contents

Introduction

The Importance of First

Although the concept of first or last may sound unfair and difficult to accept for some, in the real world—regardless of your business or career—first place is the only place that matters. It's a position that allows you to weather all storms, gets you extra attention, and has the competition chasing you—rather than the other way around. But let's face it: if you didn't compromise on any point, you would certainly rather the position of first than any other, right? Given the choice between first and any other position, we all know what's preferable.

Unlike systems or cultures where everyone gets rewarded for just participating and regardless of their efforts, abilities, or even the score—the only position that ultimately makes sense in business—and the one that earns the greatest rewards—is, of course, first. If you aren't in the dominant position in your market, then you are at risk. When economies are abound with business, the company in first position continues to gain customers and expand its size and presence while the weaker players eke out increasingly smaller gains, helped along solely by the rich nature of the market. However, when these profitable times wane, the dominant company benefits from its first-place position and grabs market share away from all the other contenders while those in every other position pay the price.

Merriam-Webster's defines the word *first* as "preceding all others in time, order, or importance." Being first to the market is not as important as being number one in your category; you don't necessarily have to be the company introducing a product to be the best choice in the buyer's mind. Order and importance are much more vital here than time. There is also a big difference between being first and third in Google search results, as evidenced by companies like first-place Intel and second-place Advanced Micro. As of December 2009, Intel had earned $32.7 billion in revenue and had $13 billion in cash, whereas Advanced Micro had $4.92 billion in revenues and $2.5 billion in cash. And consider the competition between Barack Obama and John McCain. Only a few points separated a name that has made history. Again, Barack was not first to the market; he actually came 30 years after his opponent and had much less experience. Yet he managed to win not just the number one spot, but the most powerful position in the world.

So quit compromising and being "reasonable." Let's get you fighting—every minute of every day—for the number one spot in your business. You want to be on top when the market is great and take market share when it is not.

The "Game-Changing" Economy

Businesspeople, salespeople, managers, entrepreneurs, and CEOs fear economic reductions—and understandably so. They reason (correctly) that when the economy moves into a period of major contraction, clients and customers cut back on projects, reduce spending, and worse, sacrifice quality looking for lowest-priced vendors and/or suppliers. It becomes more difficult to raise capital, close transactions, and make accurate projections that affect planning at all levels. People become filled with uncertainty and doubt that negatively impacts their ability to make decisions. These game-changing economic times can occasionally require major transitions in our skill set as well, particularly following periods of extended expansion. It is common for management teams, sales forces, and employees to be improperly equipped to transition in the game-changing economy.

It's fairly easy to observe when people's motivation and skill sets are crippled from extended periods of economic expansion. It's a lot like a professional fighter who after a series of easy bouts appears to lose his edge, his power—even his sense of the basics. People tend to become dependent on a surplus of opportunities, easy credit, and cheap money and develop an overall unrealistic attitude when the business is good and the wind is at their backs. When the market changes and belts tighten, the forces are no longer at your back but are directly blowing in your face. Every weakness in the organization is greatly magnified when times get tough. Mistakes become more costly, every transaction vital and failure becomes a real possibility for both individuals and companies that aren't able to transition within the new economy.

At the time I began writing this book, the world was entering one of the greatest economic contractions since the Great Depression. During periods of major game-changing economic shifts, people immediately find themselves scared, confused, overwhelmed, angry, hopeless about what to do, and unsure about whether there is anything they can do. During times like these, people suddenly realize that their businesses, incomes, and futures are at risk. It abruptly seems as though the world is giving each of us a giant wake-up call by screaming, *you are vulnerable and may cease to exist*!

The truth of the matter is that if you aren't number one in your category or field, then you are in a precarious and dangerous situation. If you aren't first, it pretty much doesn't matter where you are in the race, you will suffer. Times like these show us how hazardous it is to be tied to or dependent upon the economy. Instead, you want to be in such a powerful position among your group that you are able to take advantage of the existing state of affairs.

This book is about how you can advance your professional mission and goals and not just conquer but dominate the competition and the marketplace. Regardless of your product, service, or idea—and despite a challenging economy— you can be first and should always strive to be there. You must acquire a position within your company and/or career in which you are not susceptible to economic pullbacks and start thinking in terms of creating your own financial system. I don't want you ever to settle for "just getting by" or have to worry about the condition of your finances. I say to hell with the economy! I choose to improve, conquer, and prosper and will do everything possible to be *first*. This book will show you exactly how to be successful and how to own that powerful position of first. You will learn the exact actions to take in order to advance yourself, your company, and your ideas—and always come out on top.

From Easy Times to Tough Times

When economies change from being very optimistic and positive (expanding) to very difficult and negative (contracting), people respond in a variety of ways. These responses are somewhat similar to those we experience when we endure the loss of a loved one. We first engage in denial, then anger, resentment, and (for some) apathy before, finally, recovery. But those who succeed during major economic contractions find these challenges to be inspiring moments that incite new solutions and creativity.

I assure you that the economic situation is not hopeless, and you should not give up, there are exact steps and actions you can take that will guarantee you win! This is a great opportunity for those who really want to "up" their game, attitude, and responsibility levels. My mission in life for the last 25 years has been to help people who want to improve and to succeed in doing so. The most exciting part of my job is working with the exceptional people who strive to be number one and master their market.

This book takes the lessons I've learned from these people and through my own trials and tribulations to show you exactly what you will have to do to create success, regardless of what is going on with the economy. It will instruct you on how to expand, surmount, and even exploit these challenges to reach your ideal. You'll read about simple, doable, and detailed actions to help you and your business thrive, and you'll learn specifically how to seize market share away from your competitors. You will see exactly what actions you must take on a daily basis to dominate your market and create success so great that no pullback in the economy will negatively impact you. You'll no longer depend on the economic conditions in which you live and work to dictate your success or failure. You'll be able take advantage of a weakening economy, seize market share from less profitable competitors, and use the contracting events to create the financial situation you want for yourself, your company, and your family—independent of the local, national, or world economy. There are indeed substantial advantages to periods of economic contraction; once you know how to exploit these opportunities, you will grow while your competitors shrink, submit, and disappear.

If you worry that the economy will be tough for some time but still want to learn and do whatever is necessary to enhance your business's progress, then you are in for a rocket ride when you apply what you learn in this book! You certainly are not alone either; plenty of people are seeking answers during today's challenging times. However, there is a big difference between those who are looking for answers and those who are willing to actually learn and execute on the exact actions that will ensure success. Most of your friends and family may have already ceased believing that there is anything they can do, but you have not. I congratulate you for searching for the answers.

A Warning about Books

Unfortunately, most people today purchase books that they start but never finish. I believe the reasons for this are threefold: (1) the small financial investment required for a book makes it easy for us to buy them by the dozen and read very few; (2) we don't have to make a commitment to finish by a particular date; and (3) many books contain a lot of misunderstood words.

I want you to finish this book. I guarantee that if you read it in its entirety, you'll be able to create the economy and success you want for yourself, your company, and your family—and be first in your field.

So, that said, let's dissect the above-mentioned reasons. First, people approach books as though they are worth only the price they paid for them rather than seeing them for the millions of dollars worth of information in them. This book can be worth millions to you, so read it with that kind of outlook, and approach each action as though it will make you millions (because it can!)

The second reason people don't finish books is because they never pick a target date by which to finish. That is crazy to me; you would never do this with any other project, would you? The average person reads about 200 words per minute, so he or she—if not interrupted—could finish this book in less than five hours. Before I start anything—whether reading a book or building an addition to my home—I always decide upon a target date for completion. So stop reading now and commit to a "due date" for reading this book. Just write today's date and the date by which you want to finish on the inside cover.

The last reason people don't finish books is because they run into words they don't understand and often elect to stop reading the book. For this reason, I included a very extensive glossary of words in the back of this book. The glossary does not include every way in which the word can be used: just the context in which I used it in this book. Take the time to look up the meaning of every word about which you have even the slightest doubt. Remember: your success in an area depends on the degree to which you understand the terminology being used in that area!

So treat this book like it's worth millions of dollars to you; set your target date to finish, and don't gloss over any words you don't understand. Each time you read an action be sure you fully understand exactly what I am explaining in that action. While many of them may seem clear, the only reason you won't engage is because of a lack of understanding. Don't ignore or gloss over any of the actions and I assure you that you will master your markets, and this book will become a resource for not just you but everyone in your organization.

The information contained herein will see you through any recession regardless of how bad or deep it is or how long it lasts. I know because I have used these exact techniques to get me through three recessions—and I came out of each one stronger, more capable, and more profitable. I am using them at this very moment to advance my position in the market, grab market share from my competitors and actually take ground in markets I was not in before.

Doom and Gloom Is the Time to Boom

Many of the economists, pundits, and media talking heads are predicting doom and gloom and end-of-the-world scenarios with their 24-hours-a-day round-the-clock ranting and raving. They're entirely focused on the problem and who may be to blame and don't seem to offer much in the way of a solution for surviving and prospering. You have probably already experienced a slowdown, as business has been shrinking significantly in most parts of the world. Regrettably, I'm sure you are feeling the effects—and I'm sure you don't like it. In fact, I hope you don't like it, and I would encourage you to hate it so much that you are willing to do anything to fight back. Despite the fact that we're enduring a time when many people will suffer—with millions out of work, companies failing, and entire industries disappearing—it is also a time to learn and use specific strategies to turn the tide. New companies, products, and even industries are born out of economic challenges. I want you to be a person who wakes up every day wanting to be first in your industry or field, who is not victimized by what appears to be reality but who creates a new reality out of the opportunity and rubble of the old.

By taking very precise, exact, correct actions, you can combat any economic pullback and achieve any level of success you desire. You can continue to expand and conquer in your endeavors and move your goals and dreams forward, literally creating your own new economy. The truth is that it doesn't take a recession or contraction to create problems for a person's business or finances. I'm sure you know a fair amount people who weren't doing well, even during periods of economic expansion. Contractions introduce a different set of problems for everyone, and these different problems require varying degrees of willingness and thinking, along with a new set of actions. Financial hardships come about as a result of not being able to sell your products and services in quantities great enough and at prices high enough to make the business profitable and viable.

There can be a great many reasons for not being able to get your products and services into the marketplace—and even more excuses. The reality is that every business has ups and downs, and every economy has its cycles. Along the way to creating success and security, you have to make adjustments to accommodate ever-changing market conditions. It is impossible to be in business for any length of time and not experience a tough economy at some point. Some downturns will be worse than others: some long, some short, some very painful, and some just a blip. The good news is twofold: (1) there are exact and precise actions that you can take to counter any contraction and (2) contractions are excellent opportunities in which to expand and conquer market share. Use the doom and gloom to make this your time to boom!

CHAPTER

1

Four Responses to Economic Contractions

There are basically four responses people have during economic contractions—and only one that counts.

1. The Cheerleader Response: "I refuse to participate!"
2. The Old-School Response: "Nothing really has changed; let's just get back to the basics."
3. The Quitter Response: "There is nothing I can do, I just have to wait it out."
4. Advance and Conquer: "Every resource you have goes to advance and conquer while others contract and retreat."

Let me explain, as you move through each of the stages of recovery and as you build or rebuild your business, you will make choices in how you respond. Your response to the economic contraction will be a result of your beliefs and the influences of your environment. You have heard and/ or witnessed each of the four responses by your employers. Let's look at all four and examine the ones that work and any untruths that may be holding you back.

The Cheerleader Response

The first response—the "cheerleader"—simply refuses to participate. I love this attitude and in fact agree with it on many levels. However, there are two versions of this, one of which is workable and one that is not. The first suggests that you not partake in the thinking, actions, and behaviors of those agreeing with the economic contraction. While I agree that it's best not to buy into mass negativity, maintaining a totally positive—and therefore somewhat unrealistic—attitude during a time of serious contraction is, at best, a state of temporary denial. It's like you try (unsuccessfully, in most cases) to convince yourself "not to participate" and that somehow, you will be okay. I consider myself an optimistic person and believe my mental condition is critical to success, but it would be irresponsible and unworkable to suggest that the economy can be made different by mentally "pumping yourself up." You actually have to *do* something! It is hard to deny that credit has tightened, lenders are calling in credit lines, companies and individuals are spending less, and people are losing their jobs. I don't know of a company or an industry that is not experiencing some type of reduction in its revenues. Something very real is happening, and just cheering your way through it and refusing to participate will not change anything.

As I write this, 20 percent of all teenagers in this country are unemployed; so if the product or service that you sell is dependent upon that demographic, it will affect your business. Over 10 percent of the workforce is unemployed. In some locations, that number already exceeds 15 percent and is still climbing. These statistics are frightening in their own right and negatively impact those who can't find work. Add to that the financial damage caused by fear, anxiety, uncertainty, and lack of confidence, which can be more dev-astating than the actual facts and figures themselves. Auto sales are off by almost 40 percent, retail sales are hitting lows not seen in 25 years, foreclosures are hitting historical highs, massive amounts of wealth equity have disappeared with the downturn in housing prices, people have seen their 401(k)s cut in half, banks are failing at alarming rates, and credit is being frozen. Positive sayings and optimistic attitudes alone will not get us through this.

I am not trying to alarm you in any way, but operating under the impression that you can simply cheer your way out of this is unrealistic. We've received a serious wake-up call; those who respond by taking the right actions will advance, and those who sit by and do nothing will endure a lot of pain.

Let me give you an example. I live in Los Angeles, where—unlike the Gulf Coast, where I grew up—natural disasters are earthquakes, not hurricanes. The major dif-ference between these two events is that earthquakes offer no warning and last only a few seconds (rather than several hours). So let's say you live in or are visiting Los Angeles, and there's a major earthquake—an 8.5 on the Richter scale. Regardless of how good a salesperson you are, you will have a difficult time selling anyone—including yourself—on the idea that he or she should just refuse to participate. When you see and feel the ground you're standing on move for the first time in your life and watch as buildings sway, trust me, you will *not* be able to cheer this off. During moments of intense episodes like hurricanes and earthquakes, even stock market crashes and economic pullbacks, people become overwhelmed, freaked out, and tend to overreact. Typically, the first reaction to violent changes is to freeze up or retreat and for many, to simply deny the reality of what is happening. People are unprepared and unskilled to face such changes and don't want to confront the damages and discomfort they will bring.

However, denying the fact that you're experiencing an earthquake will certainly not change the fact that you should probably do something different to protect yourself and take a specific set of actions in order to ensure your safety and survival. For example, you might have to take a different route than usual to obtain food, water, and fuel since roads, bridges, communications, electricity, and the Internet will all be either jammed or not working. Literally *everything* you take for granted will be affected and most likely unavailable to you. Earthquakes occur very quickly, often without any kind of advance notice. Those who *know* how to respond to an earthquake will be able to move forward, while those who don't know what to do will automatically retreat.

Most people approach changes in the economy in the same way they do earthquakes: They simply don't prepare for them. This is the case especially after long periods of good times; people become a bit robotic and even lazy. They forget the muscle, discipline, persistence, energy, and creativity it takes to dominate. They don't know how to act when things suddenly change, so they merely *react*. Most individuals, managers, and CEOs get used to doing business in stable economies; they therefore don't know how to respond correctly when things are difficult again.

It's not uncommon to see people becoming overly "reasonable" about the actions that are necessary to sustain themselves and their companies. And when recessions happen—as they do and always will—many salespeople, managers, entrepreneurs, executives, and CEOs find that they are ill equipped and lack the knowledge to counter those economic contractions. People have all types of very strange responses when they aren't prepared for events. Many of the actions you take merely mirror the economic contraction whereby you actually react to the contraction with thoughts and actions that further deepen or worsen your situation. Most will handle the economic decline with further cuts, denial, or just outright apathy, while others (as mentioned previously) will refuse to participate. But reactions like these are the opposite of deciding to be *first* in your market and dominate your competition.

Old School Response

The second response is the classic old-school response to "get back to basics." This outlook suggests that nothing really has changed; if we would simply return to our "roots," everything would work out. I was working with a large group from an automotive company when an executive said, "Grant, nothing has really changed; we just have to get back to basics." I thought to myself, *your industry has gone from*

16 million new car sales a year to 9 million (the lowest level in 25 years). Every car dealer in America depends solely on advertising to drive traffic, something dealers will no longer be able to justify, and your sales force hasn't the first clue how to generate its own traffic. On top of that, the banks have pulled your floor plans (dealers borrow money to stock inventory), banks are tightening their lending criteria, and the media are telling people never to spend money again! And your response is to *get back to basics* when 95 percent of the people who work for you don't know what is "basic" enough in a major economic shift to make a difference?

While I support the overall concept of returning to the fundamental elements of an industry—and absolutely agree that the basics are vital to success—you can't depend on block-and-tackle if you're three touchdowns behind with only three minutes left in the last quarter. In other words, you can't make advances in business with just the basics. It is going to take some big plays in a very short period of time. The only way to flourish during an economic downturn is to take lots of unreasonable actions in order to dominate. Back to basics may only get you back to where you were—and remember, our goal here is to be *first*. This is not a time for simplistic sayings but rather for massive actions.

There are a lot of levels of "basic" to get through before you can finally get down to the most fundamental one: That which will get you traction in the changed market. It's also vital to understand that age, experience, and improvements in technology all influence what each person considers to be basic. If you sold products during the 1970s oil crisis, for instance, and another person had sold only between 1998 and 2008, your definitions of basic would be radically dissimilar. The definition of basic for the person who sells encyclopedias door to door varies greatly from that for the person who sells the hottest, in-demand technological gadget that people cannot seem to get enough of. I built my first company going door to door to businesses all over America, and I did it during a severe recession. People weren't coming to me to buy my service I had to knock on thousands of cold doors just to get people to even know me. I couldn't afford advertising or huge marketing programs, and I didn't have a sales team to do this for me. I was an unknown and unproven commodity. By going door to door I learned skills that no one can ever take from me and that would later define me in business and as a person. I have met hundreds of people that want to be public speakers and I always tell them the same thing. "It's easy; just learn how to get an audience!" But most people that want to speak to audiences are not willing to do what it takes to get the audience. People claim how good they can speak but what does it matter if there's no one to listen.

The point I'm trying to make here is that to claim that an organization just needs to get back to basics is like the "wannabe" speaker who cannot get an audience. You must get yourself and the organization focused on creating a future instead of one focused on merely getting back to doing something from the past. You must vow to do whatever it takes to get the audience and go one step further and do whatever your competitors refuse to do and then some—so that you can separate from all the other wannabes.

Things are always changing, and change requires actions beyond what is basic. If you don't change with the times, you will be left behind. To that end, even the basics change over time. While we certainly shouldn't disregard the basic principles of success, we do need to cultivate the basics we are using. Consider the fact that *the basics during times of expansion are different from those we use during contraction*—because you *can't afford to make mistakes*. When economies slow down, you cannot miss even one opportunity; you have to kick your activity way up and become much more tenacious about how you approach every interaction.

Think back to a time when you were extremely motivated to succeed and had to perform at a high level. You simply *had* to get results; therefore, you probably went beyond basic and switched to *serious* performance mode. To simply go back to the basics during periods of economic turmoil will not change the fact that you have fewer opportunities to work with, people have less money, credit is tight, fear is everywhere, and your clients will have more objections than ever to purchasing your product or service. While you will hear complaints, stalls, and reasons not to buy similar to those you heard when times were better, they will come with a different level of intensity and certainty from those upon whom your business depends.

It is a fact that many—if not most—of the people with whom you work have never sold in very difficult economies. So instructing those people to get back to basics won't prompt them to do things that are basic enough to get the results you want, much less take market share. And we aren't interested in going backward in this book. We are going forward.

During periods of economic expansion, business can become so easy that individuals and companies are often lulled into an inflated impression of their own abilities. They become conditioned to a false sense of what it takes to be profitable during extended periods of easy money, free credit, surplus opportunities for their products, and a world operating without financial cares or concerns. Then, all of a sudden, you find yourself enduring the polar opposite situation. Every individual in the workforce who wants to succeed must take a new look at what it really means to get back to basics, develop or relearn new skills, and start executing actions that most of us have not used for years and many more of us didn't even know were required.

The Quitter Response

The third type of response is expressed by quitters, the people who think there is nothing they can do and will wait out the economic downturn until things return to normal—at which time, they will get back to work again. This group will be crushed both financially and emotionally. They will go through all their cash, only to find out that economic contractions can last *much* longer than expected—in some cases, 18 months or even longer. These people will find themselves emotionally damaged from being out of the workforce; even when things normalize, they will find it more difficult to get work because they haven't actively participated for months. The quitters are basically scavengers who depend on "good" economies to provide enough cash to fund their lifestyles. They travel from region to region and work in industries that are doing well but never really advance and conquer for themselves. They are only good at picking low-hanging fruit—or easy business—and are unable or unwilling to dig for gold. They will never truly accumulate wealth because they never developed a work ethic necessary to acquire success. I would never have someone from this group of people work for me; they contaminate the rest of the organization. A quitter probably would not even pick up this book to read it, much less execute the actions in it. And if such people did buy the book, I would have offended them so much by this point that they probably would have thrown it in the trash!

Advance and Conquer

Now, the last school of thought: The advance-and-conquer response, and the one I promote as the only correct response for you to take. I encourage you to first embrace the idea that the market is different and has indeed changed and acknowledge that it will be more challenging (but by no means impossible) to sell your products and services, grow your business, or even keep a job. Know that it will require a completely unique sense of energy, work ethic, mind-set, and actions.

An economic slowdown is obviously an obstacle for both businesses and individuals but I will also show you that it is an opportunity for you. Starting a new company from scratch with just a little bit of money is very similar to going from a great economy to a very difficult one. You don't have credit, you don't have money, customers are hard to come by, and no one wants to see you. It's *tough*. The difference, however, with a major economic change is that *it isn't just happening to you*. Everyone's finances are affected, confidence is challenged, selling becomes more difficult, credit is tighter, and fewer opportunities exist. You're apt to be surrounded by negative people, complainers, crybabies, and excuse makers who have bad ideas and unworkable solutions. However—as I've stated before—economic contractions can also prove to be opportunities to gain new clients, boost sales, differentiate yourself and your company in the marketplace, and take market share. Therefore, advance and conquer, dominate those negatively impacted and take market from them! Those who are willing to learn new skills—and master and execute them with massive actions—will be rewarded in big ways that you could not accomplish when times were good. You will take control of market share while others surrender it.

I worked in my first sales job during the recession of the early 1980s. Unemployment rates were more than 20 percent and interest rates were 18 percent where I lived and worked. In hindsight, I probably should have moved, but I didn't have any money to do so. One out of four people could not buy the product I was selling due to the simple fact that they were out of work. I was lucky if seven or eight prospects showed interest in my product in a week. My survival was based on the most basic of actions: Generating opportunities and then learning how to handle all the objections, stalls, and reasons that individuals come up with not to buy. This was my learning ground, and I had nothing else for comparison.

When you don't know, you simply *don't know*. If you grow up in poverty in a remote location surrounded by other poor families, you don't know you are poor. The only people who know you are poor are the people who have more than you. You won't be aware of your state of affairs until you have something with which to compare it. You don't know until you know! When you're trying to sell during a period of economic contraction and don't have anything to compare it with, you're almost blessed by not knowing. You will do and adjust to whatever is necessary in order to succeed.

The biggest challenge most people face today is their tendency to keep comparing the current situation with yesterday's and wishing for yesterday to return. The only thing that works, though, is concentrating on the future and forgetting the past. Those who continue to compare themselves with others in the market by claiming that they're "doing better than the rest" must remember that the goal is to dominate, not compare yourself with those who are doing badly. A surefire way to make sure you never get to first place is to compare yourself with others who have no intention of ever being first.

Surviving Recessions

Since I began my career in the early 1980s, I have built three businesses and have endured—and even prospered—during periods of economic contraction. Most people reading this book have also survived tough times before; you simply might have forgotten that you *did* come through each of them. For instance, I was born during the 1958 recession that lasted two years. I survived it; in fact, I didn't even know we were having one. I survived another recession from 1960 to 1961 when I was three years old. In 1973, there was an oil crisis that lasted two years, and I worked all through school and during the summers when other people couldn't get a job. From early 1980 to 1982, the Iranian Revolution caused an increase in the price of oil around the world, leading the country into another recession. Survived it! In the early 1990s, the country experienced another recession that lasted a little over a year that included the housing bust, after which people swore they would never get back into real estate. I survived it. The year 2000, brought the collapse of the dot-com bubble, followed a year later by the September 11, 2001, attacks on the World Trade Center and Pentagon, causing tremendous economic fears around the world, especially in the United States. Survived both. This was followed by two years of accounting scandals and another contraction in our economy, which I also made it through. Then, in 2007, the world experienced the start of another major contraction, this time led by the collapse of the housing market, extending to bank collapses in the

United States and Europe. This resulted in bank failures, bankruptcies, foreclosures, and the subsequent failure of entire industries. We will *all* survive it. The question is can you thrive in it as well?

A recession, by definition, is basically a drop in the gross domestic product of a country over two quarters, or 180 days. Individuals and companies cannot actually experience a recession per se since they don't have gross domestic product. However, they can certainly experience the effects of recessions, and the degree to which they make or refuse to make adjustments will determine how well they endure it. I say all of this to give you encouragement and to remind you that you have survived, can survive, and will survive *any* economic contraction. But I do want to show you how to advance, conquer, and seize market share during these times.

While I would prefer to experience economic expansion, of course, the reality is that I have always done better during periods of contraction—as funny as that might seem. It's a bit of an odd phenomenon, but some people actually perform better when challenged because it triggers their need to survive and stimulates higher levels of performance. This in turn causes them to become more creative in the marketplace and more productive when others are throwing in the towel. So don't be hopeless. Contractions are not the end of the world; you can succeed regardless of the state of the economy.

Understand as well that economic contractions don't last forever. Those who don't quit but instead dig in and get through them will come out the other side with a better work ethic, an increased customer base, and a bigger piece of the market. And survivors are instilled with the confidence that they *can* prosper, regardless of the conditions in which they're doing business. So don't throw in the towel. Understand that you have a choice in what you do to counter a pullback. You don't have to suffer the financial consequences others will experience if you act intelligently.

I live by the following motto: "Problems are opportunities, and conquered opportunities equal money earned." Remember that when you face a problem, it's an opportunity in disguise. Stay in the game, push forward, never retreat—and look for creative ways to solve your problems. A situation you're able to overcome won't even look like a problem later; you'll simply recall a situation that just needed to be handled properly. Unfortunately, people who pull back and retreat to the point that they almost disappear during economic downturns won't remember problems this way. They respond in a habitually negative way and become overwhelmed to the point that they're essentially blind to prospects and solutions. When the market recovers, these individuals will have less money and fewer clients and will be forgotten by the marketplace, leaving their business and identity damaged. Your great advantage in this market is that less competition gives you the chance to stand out and capture market share.

What follows in this book are the tactics that you must use to ensure that your business grows, survives, and prospers during *all* times but *especially* during economic contractions. These are proven techniques that, when used exactly, will get you results. They are tried, true, tested, accurate, and precise formulas that will make your goals a reality. I encourage you to use them exactly as detailed and avoid being "reasonable" when you do.

Reason means proper exercise of the mind, sanity, the sum of the intellectual powers, and the possession of sound judgment. Being *unreasonable* here means that you won't allow yourself to be governed by or act according to reason. I don't want you to use your intellectual powers to make sense of this; after all, the world is filled with intelligent people who never do anything significant. Instead, I want you to operate as though you are without reason, without judgment—more like a madman or madwoman whose only goal is to make things happen. *Do not reason with these actions; just take them.* Do not apply your common sense when employing them. Use them in exactly the way I state them here. The biggest mistake you can make in using these techniques is to attempt to make them fit your personality or mind-set. Do *not* alter the actions in any way; you'll just end up with a watered-down version of what works.

Just last week I was working with a company and we identified an action of following up with customers that their competition would not employ. I suggested that the company follow up with customers as soon as the customer left rather than later in the day and even suggested that the salespeople follow customers home. Sounds crazy doesn't it? The management in this company protested, "There is no way this technique will work with our product or our customer demographic." I pleaded with the managers to just trust me and use the technique, and within 24 hours, they had contacted my office claiming, "Not only did it work, but our customers loved it!" The company was revitalized with new ways to expand into the marketplace. Now before you completely dismiss my actions as unworkable understand that your response alone means that others will not employ them either, which means those that take this action will no longer be competing but doing something completely different. At times like these you don't want to compete, you want to beat!

While these techniques should be applied to your marketing and selling efforts in all economic climates, you will find these are the type of strategies and thinking to get you through periods of contraction. This is where we are only thinking in terms of expansion and willing to try anything, even break agreed upon norms in order to grab business. And before you start thinking you are violating customer satisfaction with these actions know that same company experienced the highest customer satisfaction scores their company had ever attained. Customers were saying, "We have never had a company who had been willing to do more to earn our business." This way of thinking and these actions are for those who refuse to have their families, businesses, and financial futures put at risk—and are willing to do whatever it takes to be first. Trust me on this, and I assure you that you will be rewarded with success. I look forward to hearing about your journey to first and how much success you receive from the implementation of these powerful and effective recession-fighting techniques.

Exercise

Four Responses to Economic Contractions

Write down the four responses to a contraction.

1. _____
   _____
   _____

2. _____
   _____
   _____

3. _____
   _____
   _____

4. _____
   _____
   _____

Write down the names of people you know who fit each of the responses.

1. _____
   _____
   _____

2. _____
   _____
   _____

---

3. _____
   _____
   _____

4. _____
   _____
   _____

Write down examples of a time when you responded in each way and the result.

1. _____
   _____
   _____

2. _____
   _____
   _____

3. _____
   _____
   _____

4. _____
   _____
   _____

Write down which one of the responses you will commit to using and why.

_____
_____
_____

(continued)

(*continued*)

What are the six ways you will be affected during a contraction?

1. _____

_____

_____

2. _____

_____

_____

3. _____

_____

_____

4. _____

_____

_____

5. _____

_____

_____

6. _____

_____

_____

Power Base Reactivation

I'm going to start you on the path of "advance and conquer" with an asset that I know you have: a power base. Unfortunately, most people deny knowing that they even have a place of power. They truly believe that they have nothing to start with. *Not true.* Everyone has a power base; we simply don't all acknowledge or utilize it. Instead, we go backward by trying to build a business in a place where we don't already have power, with people we don't know. This is the most difficult way to form a company.

Everyone has an existing power base. The people you know—friends, family, relatives, schoolmates, past employers, existing employees, and even your enemies—are all part of it. A power base doesn't remain the same size throughout your career; it will grow (or cease to grow) depending on the amount of attention you give it. To cultivate and increase the quality of your power base, simply start with what you have. Direct and multilevel marketing companies are effective because they depend almost solely on utilizing and optimizing people's power bases. Combine a dedicated and relentless contact of power bases with great products, and you will create a corporation that profits during *any* economy. Amway, Nu Skin, Herbalife, Mary Kay, Market America, and Kangen Water are just a few examples of companies whose entire model is built on the idea that everyone has a power base; success depends on how effectively those power bases are informed about the company's products. Those who make it to these firms' top levels are not great salespeople; they are great at power base reactivation. That is why so many businesses focus so intently on customer satisfaction and knowing how much word of mouth generates future sales. Corporations tend to fail when they rely too heavily on advertising campaigns and claim commitment to customer satisfaction without organically stimulating the power base. When you effectively activate your power base, you will find people who are qualified to purchase your products and motivated to tell others.

You have to be cost effective in generating opportunities for purchasing your product or service during slow economic times. While a big corporation may be able to afford huge advertising budgets, individuals typically cannot. And while advertising can hit more people faster, it is less personal. To that end, your power base is the single most lucrative way to generate immediate business. Traditional advertising has become "the dependency" of the twenty-first century whereby the company's ability to generate business rests solely with mass advertising to people you *don't* know who may or may not be qualified or even interested in your product. A majority of advertising budgets are lost to these people. This method of contact may not be an affordable option—even for large corporations—during periods of contraction, when you truly have to watch every penny you spend.

Although reactivating your power base is very cost effective, it *does* require some degree of effort. Don't worry when you begin whether these people are qualified or even interested in your product; just make your list, then contact those on it. Remember that the people you know also know others in turn who may be more appropriate prospects. You want to reactivate every possible contact you have and get your power base to start to work for you. It's akin to mining; think of the people you know as gold, and treat them as you would a gold mine. Post a claim and work it constantly. Neglect it and you will find someone else claiming your fortunes. Worse yet, your power base can sit vacated, unattended, and ignored. The fact that you are not working your gold mine effectively does not mean it is less valuable; it just means that you aren't tapping into its immense potential.

Start getting in touch with friends, family, relatives, and past employers and take a genuine interest in them. Find out what they are doing; ask about their lives, their careers, and their families. People love to talk about themselves, and they really love it when others take interest in them. Let them know what you are doing when it comes up, but understand that *this is not a sales call*. You are simply reconnecting with someone with whom you have been out of touch.

Do not rely solely on e-mail or snail mail for this venture without first getting in touch via phone or personal visit. A phone call is more valuable than mail but can and should be followed by mail or e-mail the same day. Make it clear that the intention of your call is to catch up with those in your power base, not to sell your products or services. During all economies—good, bad, and indifferent but especially during contractions—contacts and relationships are everything. If you've ever heard the saying "It's who you know, not what you know," then you know that this is true. *You are short on people, not short on money, and the people you know either have the money you want or know people who do.* It is those people who want and need your service. So the more people you contact, the better chance you have of discovering and selling to those who are members of your target market.

Remember: People like to buy and do business with people they know and like. During times when money is tight, they are more likely to spend money (if they do so at all) on products and services from those they know and trust. You may have had the experience of running into an old friend and to your shock and disappointment discovered that they just bought the very product or service that you represent from someone else. Ugh! The pain runs deep and could have easily been avoided just by increasing the amount of contact with the people you know. You can miss these types of opportunities when things are going great—but when times are tough you can't afford to miss any business! And the reality is that you should never put yourself in this position, regardless of economic conditions, but now you don't have a choice—you have to capitalize on every single opportunity.

This process of reactivating your power base might feel a lot like going to the gym after blowing off exercise for six months. It is all new again and you are using muscles that you have not used in some time. Just like working out, once you force yourself back into the gym, and work through the pain, you will be glad you did! So just push through your resistance and know that your persistence is going to pay off, as long as you keep showing up and working out you will rebuild the muscle and in this case your power base.

The Call

So, let's talk about exactly how you are going to start reactivating your power base. How to make the call and what exactly you might say something like this:

"John, Grant Cardone here. Just thinking about you and wanted to catch up. How are things? What are you doing now? Tell me about the family, the house, the job?" This usually prompts your contact to ask what *you* are doing; at which point, you tell them and emphasize how excited you are about it. Do not, under any circumstance, mention or discuss or get involved with a conversation about how bad the economy is. No one needs more bad news!

Take the time during the call to collect data and update your files: E-mail and postal addresses, phone numbers, family and employment changes, etc. The second part of the call's purpose is to set up a time to meet in person. "Let's catch up this month over lunch. When is good for you?" You must commit to and set a time to meet with the person you're calling, because this will bring about two subsequent actions: filling your schedule and making personal contacts. Again, your purpose here is not to sell; it is simply to make contact, reestablish a bond, collect data, and set up a future meeting.

Follow up your reactivation call by sending out a letter or e-mail that same day. Do not wait until tomorrow. Build the habit of doing everything you can *now* to establish a discipline of taking massive action. End the call with something like, "Great speaking with you. I look forward to catching up with you in person." This call and a mailing will then be followed up with a personal visit—whether or not you get a commitment to a future date to meet. Either put the time you both agreed to meet on your calendar, or schedule a date for a personal visit.

Remember, these people already know you. They will probably want to reactivate as well and help you if they can. In fact, these people will admire you for reaching out to them—and will realize that this is exactly what they *should* be doing, too.

Here are a few very important *do nots* to keep in mind when reactivating your power base:

1. Do not qualify the list.
2. Do not worry about what these people are going to think because you haven't been in contact for some time.
3. Do not be reasonable with this action.
4. Do not try to make this a sales call.
5. However, do not *forget* that you are selling. The mere action of reactivating means you're selling.
6. Do not judge the results of the contact.

Your goal is to do everything possible to reconnect with the people you know, connect with others, network, and get people talking and thinking about you again. *Any attention is better than no attention.* The more people you know, the more likely you will survive—and succeed! So get going on your list of reactivations, and fill your calendar with appointments with everyone you can possibly think of.

Exercise

Power Base Reactivation

What types of people would be in your power base?

_____

_____

_____

Why would these people be easier to contact than any others?

_____

_____

_____

What is meant by "you are short on people, not short on money"?

_____

_____

_____

(continued)

(*continued*)

What are the five don'ts when reactivating the power base?

1. _____
_____
_____

2. _____
_____
_____

3. _____
_____
_____

4. _____
_____
_____

5. _____
_____
_____

Write down a complete list of people in your power base.

_____
_____
_____
_____
_____

Past Client Reactivation

If you are going to advance and conquer, you will be forced to reactivate your past clients. They are a gold mine you may have taken for granted for some time because you have been spoiled by an excess of opportunities.

Reactivating past clients means contacting each person to whom you have sold and provided a service before but with whom you are not actively working at this time. This is not an option; it must be done daily. The quickest and easiest way to do this is to create a list of past clients or customers and start personally calling them. You could enlist the help of someone to make these calls for you, but nothing will be more effective than making the call yourself.

Do not spend your time organizing or qualifying the list. Make calls, organize later, and *never* qualify. If someone has bought from you once, he or she still deserves to be contacted—regardless of the person's current financial situation. Remember: Everyone knows someone else. You might only be one contact away from the contact you need in order to make a sale.

During periods of immense economic negativity, your biggest benefit is the fact that your competitors are doing very little about the solution. This is a great scenario, and you want to take advantage of it. It's a critical time to protect your power base and past clients by staying in touch with them with even more regularity. Increasing the number of people you know will defy the common tendency to pull back, and it will ensure your expansion and survival. Disagree with your surroundings, disagree with the actions of those with whom you work and compete, and *always* disagree with being reasonable in the marketplace. *Do exactly the opposite of what those around you are doing, and more often than not, you will be assured success.*

The call itself is not a science, so do not agonize about whether you're saying the "right" thing. Remember, action counts more than anything. Don't spend time worrying that this person will be upset with you because you haven't spoken to him or her in awhile. Trust me; your customers haven't spent every day since you last sold to them wondering why you haven't called. The reality is that they have probably forgotten you—and *that* is exactly the problem. During tight times, you cannot afford to have anyone forget you. Those who get the most attention and stay top-of-mind will exit the situation stronger than their competitors!

A call to a past client would begin a lot like the call to those in your power base. You let him or her know that you're calling to catch up, and ask briefly about not only the person but also his or her family or business. Try to keep the small talk to a minimum so that you can address your other objective: "The second reason I am calling is to see if there is anything I can do for you at this time to enhance the investment you made with us."

Continue by asking questions about how your product is working, what the client is satisfied with, and whether there is anything that he or she is *not* satisfied with. This creates opportunities for you to be of service. And while some might suggest that asking for problems gets you problems, my experience has demonstrated time and time again that problems are opportunities for you to shine. They give you a chance to either solidify the relationship and pull farther away from the competition or actually increase your business by replacing the problem with new products or services. Go into full-service mode when you're faced with a customer issue to solve; it will bring you back into regular communication with a client with whom you've lost touch. Remember: *Contacts turn into contracts, and the more contacts, the more contracts.* Embrace the challenges that others avoid and use them to create opportunities to propel yourself, your products, and your services.

When ending an activation call with a past client, always reiterate your original reason for calling:

"If there is anything we can do for you, let me know. By the way, what is your best mailing address? I need to send you something." (Make sure you get it!) "Great. And what is your current e-mail address?" Again, don't get off the phone without gathering this information; you will use it in your follow-up mailing and personal visit. Do not evaluate the success of the call based on what happens. Simply acknowledge the fact that you have reactivated an old client—something that is going to be helpful in the future as you continue to contact clients via phone calls, mailings, e-mails, and personal visits.

There is another, more aggressive approach that you can take. It would start the same way as the previous call:

"John, Grant Cardone here. How are you? Hey, I'm calling you for two reasons: First, I haven't spoken with you in some time and wanted to catch up. How are you, the family, and your business?" (Again, keep this short, unless the person wants to talk.)

Then you would discuss information that's more specifically tailored to this particular client:

"The second reason I am calling is that I was looking at your account, and I realized that we've just introduced some special programs that could move you up in product line without changing your monthly expense. Would that be of interest to you?" (This technique is called "improve the client's situation.")

The moment I notice any type of contraction in the economic cycle, I have a set of actions I immediately deploy, one of which is to increase communication with existing clients by offering to improve their situation. I don't wait until the media begin talking about how bad things are getting in the market; I proactively look for the cycles, and then take action before things get too out of hand. Your clients will automatically look for ways to reduce expenses during down times. I see this as an opportunity and start contacting clients with an offer to replace or add to their current product or service and reduce their monthly payments by extending their contract.

For instance, my firm sells long-term training and consulting contracts to businesses. Companies typically hire us, we agree on a price and then sell the contract to a third party, and the client then pays installments to a third party (finance company) for a set period of time. Let's say a previous client has six months left to pay to the third party. We then get on the phone and call our client in order to renew the training contract before it matures, add training dates that the client is going to need anyway, and carry the balance owed over to a new contract with revised dates and terms, thereby reducing the customer's payments. The client gets the training he or she needs at a lower monthly payment, and we get revenue and continue to service our client in a contracting market. It is most definitely *win-win*. But you have to think in creative terms of how to move your clients forward and reactivate them with new products and services.

Of course, not every client will take us up on our offer, nor is every client even qualified to do so. But this creative thinking and acting allows us to stay in frequent contact with customers and puts us back in the game.

I'll bet you are trying to figure out how you can apply these scenarios to your business. Steps like these require that you take responsibility for all the parts of the cycle, aspects of which you might not have considered to be your responsibility in the past. You will not just be doing your job; you will be making sure all the other pieces get done as well. You have to do more than sell and promote when things get tough. You will be forced to assume control of all the tasks associated with gaining a client and getting the job done. There are probably fewer people in your organization now and you will have to take on more of a responsibility for each of the steps necessary to conquer business. Remember many of your work associates will be stuck in some other stage of recovery maybe even apathy so don't count on them to respond with the same "attack" mentality that you do.

Also do not get lost in the details. In the case of lowering someone's payments as I suggested in the previous example, do not concern yourself with whether you can deliver on the absolute idea of reducing your clients' payments or providing a service at no cost but that the critical goal is to determine interest and open a sales cycle. "No cost" or "lower payments" are relative terms that mean something different to everyone. To the degree that your client displays interest and sees value in the offer, he or she will justify taking you up on it—or not. Don't focus solely on how to close a transaction with this contact; just concentrate on reactivating your existing clients and creating interest in your products and services. The opportunities will validate themselves.

If the contact expresses an interest, that's good, of course. But if not, simply return to the service part of the call:

"Well, thanks for taking the time to talk with me! Again, the main reason I called was to see if there is anything I could do for you to enhance the purchase you made with us." End the call with, "Let me know if there is anything I can do for you. And by the way, I would love to catch up with you sometime over lunch."

You don't have to ask for business directly, but you do need to make contact. Second in importance to initiating the call is how you end it. It is vital to return to the original reason for calling and end on the positive, service intention of the call.

As with all calls you make, follow up this call with a letter, then set a time to make a personal visit. Combine the use of available technology like customer relationship management (CRM), database management, computer programs, data-scrubbing programs, and even electronic proposals with the phone, e-mails, social networking, and don't forget personal visits to maximize your follow-up. The mail and Internet can be very powerful ways to stay in touch, but don't rely on one or the other. For example, I created a computer program for automobile dealers that took the negotiating process away from the salesperson. The program, called EPencil™ electronically generates the entire proposal and gives the company and presenter more credibility, speed, and delivery capabilities. The company can then use these electronic proposals to control and improve the sales experience as well as market its products in its mail programs, Internet responses, traditional advertising, and direct-mail offers.

Warning: *Reactivating past clients has to be approached from a standpoint of offering service and taking interest in the client.* Again, it is not a sales action. You should expect one order or assignment for every 10 to 12 calls you make. While this approach may not achieve a high return per call, it is essential to fully farming the opportunities you have already identified. You have invested a lot in these clients already, so continue to put forth time, energy, and effort toward those relationships that have already paid off. After all, you wouldn't enter a gold mine and get a few ounces without going back in to gather the rest of the lode. The same holds true for your client list. Treat your clients like gold, and continue to mine by reactivating your relationships.

For those readers who are most "unreasonable" and dedicated: Take the earlier calls and add a referral component whereby you create an opportunity to have the old client replace him- or herself with another. After you've made some small talk and checked on the product, ask the following: "Who do you know who might be in the market for our product?" Personally, I would do this for every call, but I am a completely unreasonable individual who knows from experience that you only get what you ask for. And contrary to popular but misguided belief, asking for referrals cannot negatively affect you. It will in fact *improve* your clients' perception of you as a professional. I am doing what every businessperson knows should be done—something that will be discussed in detail later.

Again, do not call and talk about how bad the market is or tell a client that you're calling because things are slow. No one wants to hear more of this. Be positive, be assertive, be in control, and be of service.

Now, let's get into action. Pull up five clients from your database who bought from you in the first quarter of last year and make the call. No organizing, no coffee; just make the call. Don't be scared, and don't think about what you are going to say or what they might say; just go for it. The faster you do it, the less you will be intimidated! Remember, most of what you fear in life never happens. And if you don't have five clients from last quarter because this is your first quarter, either find five from some period of time or identify those who bought from someone who previously worked at your company.

Always keep in mind that your purpose during this call is to offer clients solutions or improve their situation in some way. If you have a complete commitment to succeeding, surviving, advancing, and taking market share, then ask for a referral.

Exercise

Past Client Reactivation

Why do you want to approach this contact with interest as a service action, *not* as a sales action?

_____

_____

_____

Why should you avoid overorganizing before this call?

_____

_____

_____

(continued)

(*continued*)

Why would you want to solicit problems?

_____

_____

_____

How will you add a referral component to your call?

_____

_____

_____

Want to increase your level of action?

Visit www.grantcardone.com/resources

CHAPTER

4

The Most Effective Call to Advance and Conquer

Personal visits are the single most powerful method by which you will ever make contact with a client and are *guaranteed* to advance your position in the marketplace. It would take 10 phone calls to equal the outcome of one personal visit. I built my seminar and speaking business under the assumption that making personal visits to clients—who did not even know me—is the best way to grow a company. I was in Memphis one week and stopped by three clients to say hello after my seminar, something that has a powerful effect on both them and me. When I was building my first business, there were instances—frequent ones, in fact—when I simply wasn't able to get an appointment to see someone. So I opted to make personal "cold" visits to make myself known. It was the scariest thing I have ever done, but because I wasn't known and had no capital for advertising, it was the only way I could introduce myself and my company to those with whom I wanted to do business.

Establishing personal contacts is an incredibly effort-intensive action. It takes lots of guts, but it will help you develop skills that you won't be able to hone unless you repeat them over and over again. This habit has had more to do with my personal and business success than any other approach I have ever taken. In addition to helping establish a client base, personal contact will elicit in clients a level of confidence in you that is not attainable in any other way. Master this skill and you will be able to care for yourself and your family and build a business *anywhere*.

Making personal visits can also help you overcome the fears and insecurities you might feel with regard to your abilities. It certainly did for me. It forced me to disregard many of the so-called business protocols that I believe denied me success.

The president of the United States does not become the president *without* making personal visits, shaking hands with those he doesn't know, and kissing lots of babies. He or she is required to reach out—welcomed or not—and make contact at his or her own personal risk. Any successful politician will tell you that neither money nor speeches can replace reaching out personally and touching people. If it is good enough to make a person president, then it is certainly good enough for me. And believe it or not, you *are* running for president—president of *your* industry and marketplace. Okay, so it's not a public office recognized by other countries. It's a private office over which you have 100 percent authority and no one else to blame. There's no congress or senate to appease. You are in complete control of your economy, and your approval rating is not an issue. There's no media attacking your every move. You get your way in any situation, and you alone determine the conditions of your universe. As president, the personal visits you make to the people with whom you have done business before will ensure the health, solvency, and success of your administration.

I am not suggesting that you grow your business solely on making personal calls the way I did mine, because you likely have two things going for you that I didn't: (1) your power base (people you know); and (2) your past customers. Use the power of personal visits with those two sources first before you start making cold calls, I will show you exactly how to most effectively do that.

My wife is an actress, and one time, after she returned from an audition that didn't go well, I tried to console her. She responded by informing me, "You have no clue what it's like to go on an audition." I told her, "Sweetie, I understand. I have been on more auditions in my life than you and 10 other actors combined, with only two differences: (1) I call it a sales call; and (2) I was never invited."

When you want something bad enough, you will do whatever it takes to make it happen—including ignoring social norms and acceptable behaviors in order to get your products and services known. *The marketplace—particularly in a contracting market—will only reward those who are willing to do whatever it takes.*

Remember: You're going to use the information collected during your "checking-in call" on this personal visit. It's not a cold call because these people are friends, relatives, and even former clients and contacts. There are a lot of reasons why people don't make this call. One of them is that we are socialized *not* to go to extreme measures in order to get what we want in life. You and I are basically programmed to be reasonable and logical (suppressed in this case) rather than unreasonable, illogical (which is good in this case) and willing to do whatever it takes to create success. This is the main reason why people do not make their dreams come true.

The economy does not have to be in dire straits in order for people to have financial problems. You see proof of this every day. Economies, therefore, don't determine success; your actions do. Economies don't run people; people create and run economies. Individuals and companies suffer because they refuse to do *whatever it takes*. People suffer financially because they are unable and unwilling to get in front of enough people in order to promote themselves, their services, and their products. Have you ever seen a guy dating a beautiful woman who is seemingly "out of his league" and wondered, *how did he do that*? Well, he was unreasonable and disregarded the things that most people consider important. And because of that, he got the pretty girl.

Personal contact is both the most effective and most feared kind of all sales calls. It is also the *fastest* way to separate yourself from your competition. You must be willing—especially during economic slowdowns—to take extreme actions in order to offset the pullback. Often, the action only *seems* extreme because people are conditioned to wait for something to happen rather than *make* something happen. I have never met anyone who doesn't agree that nothing is more effective than personal contact when trying to sell yourself, your product, or a service. Since entire industries have become addicted to mass marketing and huge advertising programs, they have become dependent upon taking orders instead of creating opportunities. Advertising is ineffective during periods of contraction, however, as it becomes unaffordable and falls on deaf ears. Members of the public are only looking for products that will save them money with no investment! Full-page ads are put in the trash and never read. Billions of e-mails go unread every-day because they end up in junk mail folders. Personal visits, on the other hand, are cost effective, targeted, and a major way of differentiating yourself in the marketplace. They will get potential customers thinking about you and your company.

I want you to make one personal visit a day for the next 21 days—and watch your life and business become revital-ized. From the people you called or sent mail to in the two actions I mentioned earlier, choose one person a day with whom to make a personal visit. Do not call and tell that per-son you are coming by; do not ask for permission. Just drop in. In most situations, you will likely meet the gatekeeper/receptionist, at which time you will say, "Is John in? I am a personal friend." (Or "He is a client of mine.") "I was in the neighborhood and just wanted to say hello." If your client is not in, leave your card and take the time to pay attention to the person who greeted you. He or she should become a new addition to your power base because you will need him or her for future contacts with your client.

On those occasions when you do get face to face with your contact, simply say, "John, I was in the neighbor-hood and wanted to stop by and say hello. Do you have a few minutes? How are things? Is the product or service you bought from me satisfying you?" In the case of a past client with whom you have yet to be successful: "I was in the neighborhood and wanted to stop by and see how you are doing and take some time to reconnect. How is your business? How is the family?"

The clients you meet will naturally reciprocate and ask about what you are doing. Respond in kind, and if they express interest and you see an opening, do some fact-finding to see how you can help them. If there is no fit for what you do, ask them for the name of someone they know who might be able to use your services. You might say, "I didn't come by for this, but who do you know that would be interested in using my products or services?" Then be quiet and let the client think about it and give you a name.

There is no downside to a visit. No one will throw you out, no one will ridicule you, and no one is going to call the police on you. There is no way to be rejected or even fail, as you are basically just dropping by to say hello and reconnect; you're not trying to sell anything. The upside is that you may get lucky and run into someone who actually needs what you have, which will allow you to enter into a presentation, a proposal, and a sale. If you just sit around and wait for something to happen to you, you will be doing a lot of waiting—and will be miserably disappointed at the end of the month.

If you go out and start making things happen, something *will* happen. This is one of the great underused methods for surviving a contraction. Consider the person who loses his job and is looking for work. Most people spend time rebuilding their résumés and then send them out and wait for someone to look at them. When the economy slows down, jobs are lost, and more people need work. This means that more résumés are being sent to companies, which decreases the chance of yours being read. You won't get a job with just a résumé; it will happen when you get in front of someone, meet that person, and make him or her feel confident about hiring you. I am shocked at how much more time and money people spend on figuring out how to write a résumé than on how to sell themselves during an interview.

Look around your office. Do you see money or opportunities to do business? Mostly likely, you don't because these things only exist *outside* your office. Similarly, if you run a company from home, you won't find any hidden money in your kitchen. No one who lives there is going to buy your products or services or fund your projects. So start with your power base and past clients. Reach out to them by way of personal visits. Thousands of businesses—even entire empires—have been built by such means. Get over your hesitation and resist any of the beliefs you have been taught. Become unreasonable, and act like your life depends on doing this one thing well.

So go make a personal visit—either right now or first thing tomorrow. I don't care who it is you go see; just go. Then schedule a visit every day for the next 21 days. If you don't miss a day, making such connections will become a habit by that time, and you will be experiencing the rewards of advance-and-conquer techniques.

Exercise

Most Effective Call to Advance and Conquer

Why are personal visits more effective than any other type of contact?

_____

_____

_____

Which two groups are the first you will see on your personal visits?

1. _____

   _____

   _____

2. _____

   _____

   _____

Why is there no money in your office? Where is it?

_____

_____

_____

What are the four things that will not happen to you as a result of making a personal call?

1. _____

   _____

   _____

2. _____

_____

_____

3. _____

_____

_____

4. _____

_____

_____

To whom could you easily pay a personal visit today?

_____

_____

_____

Want to know how to be 100 percent?

Visit www.grantcardone.com/resources

Converting the Unsold

Take a moment to think about all those people with whom you have worked but to whom you have not sold anything. It's probably a huge number because the reality is that you don't sell to most of the people you work with. We are now going to take every person who has landed in this category over the last six months and convert the "unsold" into the "sold." Though rarely utilized, this tactic truly works; after all, don't these people remain unsold simply because you didn't transact with them? Everyone ends up doing *something*; it is just a matter of when and with whom. The fact that you failed to close an opportunity and then dropped or forgot about that lead does not mean that person is no longer potentially in the market for your services. Just because you quit following up or the client bought from someone else doesn't exclude that person as being a prospect for you now. Maybe he or she couldn't afford your product at the time, wasn't quite ready, or delayed a decision with the intent to reconsider. Maybe the client couldn't get funding at the time, maybe you had the person on the wrong product, or maybe he or she bought from someone else and isn't happy with that decision.

This greatly overlooked opportunity must be converted so that you can advance and conquer. Don't waste time worrying about the fact that you didn't sell to these potential clients before. They still represent a viable opportunity and should not be written off as part of past experience or as "losses." Rather, they should be reactivated until they become a future sale or a part of your ever-expanding power base. Such prospects are great people to add to your "personal drop-by" call list. Remember, everyone knows others—and the more people you are connected with, the more people you will know and will know you!

A study by Thomas Publishing Company reveals that most salespeople, regardless of the industry, give up too early. According to the study, 80 percent of sales to businesses are made on the fifth sales call, but only 10 percent of salespeople call beyond three times. *Oops!* Chances are that you haven't followed up on leads diligently enough, consistently enough, or long enough. The new business you need is sitting safely away in your files. Since you've already invested the time and energy, just keep following up and chipping away until you mine the gold. The best way to do this is to go back through your notes or database. Use the earlier actions discussed, and never rely on one means of contact. Bring all of your artillery to your acquisition of new clients—including phone calls, messages, mail, e-mail, and personal visits and never stop following up. I have clients that I have called everyday for 20 days consecutively before they finally took my call. Regardless of the reason they are not calling me back, when it comes time to doing something with my product, I will be the one they think of first. Is that too much? Not if you want to be first!

Here is an example of a call you can make to people with whom you worked in the past but did not close a sale: "John, Grant Cardone here. We met four months ago when you were considering my product. While we were not successful in earning your business at that time, I wanted to call today for two reasons. First, I wanted to check on you. How are you?" (Engage in small talk, but not forever.) "Second, where are you today with what you were considering four months ago? Did you ever make a purchasing decision?"

If the person has not bought from you, conduct new fact-finding as though you haven't before. You will need to start this sale over from scratch. Do not assume that what the client previously wanted is consistent with what he or she needs or wants now. Ask the person what has changed since then. Inquire as to why he or she opted not to do anything at that time. Then ask, "What are you looking to accomplish now?" This sales cycle may come back to life and require you to start new fact-finding, launch a new presentation, possibly introduce a completely different product, and present a brand new proposal. *Do not shortcut any of your sales steps because you did them earlier.* Start this entire sale over and disregard anything that you've done before; it is no longer pertinent.

If the contact bought from someone else, congratulate him or her. Ask how the product is working, and let the contact know that you're there to help if there is anything you can do to serve him or her. Say something along the lines of, "I would be happy to help you regardless of where you bought. I regret that I was unsuccessful in earning your business." Remember: Every contact is more valuable than just the one sale. This person will buy again and likely knows others who will buy. Again, the only difference between a contact and a contract is the relationship. The competitor who was lucky enough to get this person's business is probably no longer following up with him or her, which puts you head and shoulders above the person who won the previous sale.

Remember to follow up every call with a letter, and put this individual on your list of personal contacts and your intended visits on your calendar. Continue to nurture these "lost" opportunities until they join the ranks of your client list. Don't forget that these people are part of your power base, even though you have not sold to them (yet). I once had a prospect in Washington, D.C., whom I called twice a year. I failed one year after another to earn his business. But I continued to treat him as a client and call him regularly, and after *10 years* of persistence, I finally earned his business. It was one of the biggest contracts I ever landed. As Vince Lombardi accurately stated, "Winners never quit, and quitters never win!"

Converting unsold leads can be profitably used on prospects who have inquired about your product or service within the last year or two—sometimes even three years ago or longer. However, the best prospects would probably be those who contacted you within the past six months. I personally don't set time limitations when reactivating. A contact from three years ago is no more or less valuable to me than one made three days ago. What is of value to me is the *individual*—the nature of the previous relationship; his or her name, phone number, and e-mail address; and where I can go to make personal contact. I find that as many as 50 percent of the prospects I contact will encourage me to send literature and show some level of interest in my products or services. Of those, maybe 20 percent will be buyers in the same period. Follow up, follow up, follow up. Persistence always pays off.

However, you must be creative in continuing to follow up in this manner. You cannot merely focus on selling your product. I have had people tell me, "Grant, you are wasting your time." Yet I still continued with my commitment and followed up because I didn't believe that I was wasting my time; I was *investing* it and doing the job necessary. Whether it meant making another call, sending a piece of mail or an e-mail, paying a personal visit, or figuring out where a client was going to be at a certain time so I could coordinate bumping into that person, I continued to follow up.

Make the decision that no one is going to sway you from doing your job and taking the actions necessary to create the business you want. I know it may seem a bit extreme, but you and I are not looking for approval. We want to grow our businesses. Americans have this incredible aversion to anger and treat it as unwanted. Other cultures put a lot less meaning on strong emotions and recognize them as just being part of the exchange that takes place. Sometimes people get heated; it doesn't mean you shouldn't continue the transaction and consummate a deal.

A successful Los Angeles businessman named Kevin Kaul told me, "The difference between a contact and a

contract is the relationship, and if you don't continue contact, you will never create the relationship necessary to turn
the contact into a contract." To really be in a relationship
means that you are in it during good times and bad. After
all, the fact that my wife and I have a disagreement doesn't
mean I wouldn't ever talk to her again. Yet businesses,
management, entrepreneurs, and salespeople make this mistake every day. They fail to follow up because of some perceived negative emotion, communication, or lack of interest
on the part of the prospect. Some appear concerned that if
they follow up too persistently, they may be labeled as des-
perate. However, becoming overly concerned about a label
like this means that most people never do what is necessary
to be labeled highly successful.

To help make sense of pushing through uncomfortable moments, try to determine what the benefit will be
when the uncomfortable action pays off. Let's say you
want a client who is worth $100,000 to your company and
$10,000 to you—in addition to job security and a sense of
accomplishment. Ask yourself, "Is it worth going through
the discomfort of continuing to follow up—even after I
have been told no—in order to have any hope of getting
this done?" If you don't follow up, you will not get the
sale. If you do, you might! A client once told me, "I never
do business with anyone the first three times they call on
me. Most I won't even see. I figure if they don't believe in
their product or service enough to keep following up, why
should I waste my time to see them the first time?"

I was once involved in a very large transaction in which all parties thought we had an agreement except for me. I simply was not satisfied with the price I was being paid even though everyone else, including my partners, were very happy. While I knew a renegotiation would be ugly and create a lot of negative emotions, I also knew that if I didn't renegotiate, I was always going to regret it. I elected to renegotiate despite everyone's advice, and while it did get very hairy and emotional, we did not lose the deal— and increased our sales price by almost $12 million. I know you're sitting there saying to yourself, "Sure, I would do it for twelve big ones." But you need to start building the muscle and discipline to follow up and do the uncomfortable things on a smaller scale because these difficult actions will prepare you for big transactions. *Follow up, follow up, and follow up—despite what anyone tells you, despite the emotions, despite anything—follow up!*

Another example of the importance of persistence: I recently had someone show an interest in my company's services, but when we started to follow up with information and pricing, he seemed to lose interest. I started calling him back and spoke with him briefly on two occasions. Since then, neither my staff nor I have been successful getting him back on the phone. I've left 30 messages on his business and cell phones and have sent him at least 18 e-mails. All this was done over a period of six weeks, with each call and e-mail communicating a high degree of interest in him and his company and with me clearly stating, early on, that

I would continue this type of activity no matter how long it took. We also sent him six videos and six sales strategies via e-mail that he could use for his business. Now, keep in mind that he responded to only 3 of the 52 transmissions sent to him, none of which took place after the first week. You might think by his lack of response that he was not interested. However, I did not believe that *his* interest was as important as *my* interest in him. Just as I was concluding this chapter, he e-mailed me asking for information on me and my company relative to providing him with support for the upcoming year.

The lessons to be learned:

1. Commit to follow up.
2. Your interest in your clients is more important than their interest in you.
3. State, up front, that you will continue to follow up until you get a result.
4. Be creative in the ways that you follow up.
5. Always, always, always leave a message on recorders and voice mail.
6. Never quit, ever! Be unreasonable in your follow-up, and you will gain market share regardless of the economy.

Exercise

Converting the Unsold

What are the seven reasons why someone might not have purchased from you?

1. _____

_____

_____

2. _____

_____

_____

3. _____

_____

_____

4. _____

_____

_____

5. _____

_____

_____

6. _____

_____

_____

7. _____

_____

_____

(continued)

(*continued*)

What do the statistics say about how many times you need to call on someone before you get a deal?

_____

_____

_____

What are you warned to do in case the "lost sale" shows interest?

_____

_____

_____

Explain what is meant by "your interest in them is more important than their interest in you."

_____

_____

_____

What are the benefits to always leaving a message?

_____

_____

_____

What are the vital points or lessons learned regarding follow-up?

1. _____

_____

_____

2. _____
_____
_____

3. _____
_____
_____

4. _____
_____
_____

5. _____
_____
_____

6. _____
_____
_____

Want to learn how to convert the unsold?
Visit www.grantcardone.com/resources

6

Multiply through Existing Clients

If you are directly involved with sales—or if you own a company that sells a product—then you've probably received a call at one time from an existing client introducing you to someone he or she knew who wanted your product or service. Unfortunately, this is something that happened *to* you, not *because of* you. The goal is to *make* this happen more often so that you aren't waiting and hoping. Anyone can get lucky, but you want to use your actions to create luck.

Waiting around is a low-level, apathetic, passive activity that lets too many unknown factors rely on chance. You want to be—as often as possible—the generator of any activity for your business because then you will control the outcome and income regardless of the economy in which you live and work. I actually have this crazy idea that if you're involved in an accident, it is better to *cause* it than have it happen to you. When most people get into an accident, the first thing they do is start pointing fingers, shouting (unconsciously) to the world that he or she is a victim. At least when you cause the accident, you can say, "I made that happen."

I would rather be the cause than the effect. I would rather make a bad investment decision than give someone my money and have *them* make a bad investment decision. I hate being a victim, and I don't trust or want to wait on that thing called luck. I don't mind failing as long as I am failing because I go for it, and I don't mind mistakes if they're mistakes I made while *doing* something as opposed to something happening to me. The goal of these steps is for you to *take actions* that will generate additional opportunities and revenue and ultimately help you create your own economy.

Let's return to the concept of using existing clients to create new clients. There are two things you must do: (1) always ask; and (2) concentrate on *how* you ask. While I discussed this briefly in an earlier chapter, I now want to focus on the specific contact and technology whereby I ask existing clients to reactivate others they know and help me build my business.

You will call *all* of your existing clients and touch base to see if there is any way you can further serve them. You'll offer suggestions on how they can better maximize the product or service you sold them, and before ending the call, you'll ask *them* to help *you*. "John, let me ask you—do you have any friends, family, or business associates who would have a use for or an interest in the products and services I represent?" Then be silent and let him tell you. If he says he doesn't know anyone, say, "I understand. If you did know someone, who might it be?" It might sound confusing, but you will be *shocked* at how many times this second question will generate names. You will also be surprised how many times you get a name the first time you ask. Some clients will even say, "Funny you should ask. I was talking to so-and-so today and he asked me where I got mine." Then respond with, "Great! How do you spell his last name? First name? At what number can I reach him? What is his e-mail address? And why do you think he would be interested?"

Do not ask, "Will you give him my name?" *Do not* ask, "Can you give me his name?" *Do not* ask, "Do you know his number?" You want to ask these specific questions above—not for your client's permission. Be sure to inquire as well, "Why did you think of him?"

Business consultant and very bright business development expert Tom Stuker once said, "The worse part of earning a client's business is that you lose your best prospect." It is *critical* that you replace those to whom you sell with new prospects; otherwise, you will always find your personal production going up and down. Your success is not limited by the economy; it's only limited by the people you know and the amount of interest you can generate in your products and services. This is how you create your own wealth without depending upon the national or global economy. Salespeople, managers, entrepreneurs, CEOs, businesses, and entire industries suffer and even cease to exist because they don't take the time to generate new opportunities from those they just conquered. As I stated before, you cannot advertise your way through an economic contraction. You simply have to do a better job of working, creating, and finding every possible contact who might do business with you!

Learn how to activate and multiply your existing clients to create new ones. Trust me, they will help you if you ask. Ask early and often in the relationship—and *keep* asking. I have never paid clients for this kind of help, but I have rewarded them after the fact. I deliver a great product, service the hell out of it, do everything I can to create a "wow" experience—and then *shamelessly* ask the people to whom I have sold if they know anyone interested in what I have to offer. I have even used this method with people who haven't bought from me. I remember asking one particular client who I was unable to close a deal with, "Who do you know that would be interested in taking advantage of what I'm offering you?" He said to me, "Why would I send you to my competition? I don't want them to improve." Then, for no apparent reason, he reversed his earlier lack of interest and said, "If you believe in what you do that much that you would ask for a referral after I turned you down; then come in and do a full presentation for me and my team!" Now, I have no idea why he suddenly changed his mind. Maybe he took a minute to consider exactly *why* he would not want to send me to someone else—even when he himself had just denied my services. All I know is that for some reason, that single question changed his mind. I presented to his group, and he became a great client who subsequently hooked me up with others in his sphere of influence, thereby opening the door to other clients for me.

I've also had people opt not to do business with me but give me the names of others who they thought might want to at that time. I've even earned a referral's business before closing a deal with the person with whom I was originally working!

Famed clergyman and writer Basil King is quoted as saying, "Be bold, and mighty forces will come to your aid!"

The actual saying was, "Go at it boldly, and you'll find unexpected forces closing round you and coming to your aid." From the Bible, John 16: "Ask and you shall receive." Well, the same truths apply in business as they do in life since life comprises business and its quality depends—in many ways—upon the quality of your business. The only rule when it comes to generating opportunities is that you must generate and regenerate as many imaginable in order to prosper. So be relentless in your commitment to drive new possibilities to your business.

Don't ever allow yourself to be misled by those who suggest that asking your customers for help could in some way endanger the relationship or their perception of you and somehow damage "the customer satisfaction experience." American business seems to have made customer satisfaction its mantra under the misguided belief that a company that says the phrase enough will somehow magically gain market share. It's as though companies have over-emphasized the goal of customer satisfaction to the point that they are neglecting how vital it is to attain customers in the first place. Markets are too competitive and too fluid; you have to get the customer's attention first before you can worry about satisfying them. Of course, we all want loyalty, but first, you must get a customer.

There is an almost endless list of these customer satisfaction–obsessed companies that are now unfortunately unable to deliver *any* level of satisfaction because their doors are closed. Washington Mutual, Circuit City, Heard Automotive, and Dillard's are just a few of the organizations that spent hundreds of millions of dollars on customer satisfaction ads (mere rhetoric) and never delivered. The number of companies around the world that have changed their names to include words like "Friendly" or "Courtesy" in an effort to repair damaged perceptions astounds me. Changing your name won't keep you in business any more than an advertisement that says you deliver great customer satisfaction will make satisfied customers. If you don't know how to attain a customer in the first place and sell that person your services, you need not even bother with customer satisfaction!

Without new opportunities to replace previous prospects-turned-customers, you cannot survive in the market; you won't be in business to deliver service, much less satisfaction. I encourage you to put customer attainment before everything and to follow it immediately with a *true* commitment to customer satisfaction. You must activate clients, close deals with the clients, replace the clients with new prospects, and make sure you exceed their expectations—in that order. A business owner with whom I worked once told me, "You can't ask a client for a referral before you've even earned the right to do business with them." I railed on him with a barrage of questions: "Who told you I can't do that? Where is the rule or protocol that says you cannot do this? Who is giving you this kind of suppressive advice? Do you want to grow your business or shrink it?" I then calmed down and told him, "I know the Ten Commandments, and that isn't one of them! The rules and limitations you are playing by are in your mind and have no place in your business." This man's business was failing because he was being *overly reasonable* in his commitment to create new opportunities.

In the 25 years that I have been in business, I have never had a customer become upset with me because I asked for a referral, and I have asked during, before, and after the transaction—perhaps *too* often. So make an unwavering and unreasonable commitment to activate your clients in order to generate new opportunities for yourself, and I assure you that you will expand, conquer, and take market share away from your competitors.

Exercise

Multiply through Existing Clients

Why is it better to cause something to happen rather than have something happen *to* you?

_____

_____

_____

What are the exact questions you should ask when requesting a referral?

_____

_____

_____

(continued)

(continued)

What are the three things to avoid when asking if your client knows someone who might need your business?

1. _____
   _____
   _____

2. _____
   _____
   _____

3. _____
   _____
   _____

What is the right way to ask?

1. _____
   _____
   _____

2. _____
   _____
   _____

3. _____
   _____
   _____

CHAPTER

7

Delivering at "Wow" Levels

Ask yourself whether anyone has delivered you a truly "wow" experience within the last 90 days. I expect the answer from most of you will be no. People today are so accustomed to poor or mediocre service—both before and after the sale—that when they get something a few notches above mediocre, they are certain to notice the difference. It's very rare for people to deliver at levels that really create an exceptional experience and positive impression. Ask yourself what percentage of the time you even remember the person who served you. If you did remember them, what percentage of the time did you remember them because they "sucked"? I would expect that you *don't* remember more often than not—and when you do, it's because it was a bad experience, not a good one.

This is a perfect follow-up to my discussion on customer satisfaction in the previous chapter. You have to do everything you can to hold on to your existing clients at all times because they represent the foundation on which you grow your business. Without positive word of mouth, you have no chance of sustaining yourself—much less conquering market share. And the best way to retain your clients or customers is to please them beyond their expectations and to keep doing so—before, during, and after the sale. If you truly want to satisfy them, make sure they're impressed *before* the sale; otherwise, you won't have a chance to impress them later!

While this is always the case, it is especially critical that you deliver at a whole new level during a period of contraction in order to differentiate yourself because (1) you cannot afford to miss opportunities; and (2) this is the time to take market share from others. You don't want customers just to be satisfied; you want them wow-ed!

The wow experience is actually easier to accomplish during "bad" times than good, because your competitors are so locked up on problems during down times that their ability to deliver a positive experience has likely deteriorated. They become victims of the economy because they have no intention of creating their own economy or understanding of how to create one, and they perpetuate these declining conditions without even thinking in terms of wow. It becomes very difficult and maybe impossible for them to think in terms of wow when they are completely committed to "woe is me." It is essential that you go above and beyond to impress consumers when they tighten up financially and become more selective. Delivering a wow experience gives you a much better chance of separating them from what they are being told is so precious and vital to their survival: their money. With the media's constant reminders of doom and gloom during times like these, the wow part of an experience is the only thing that prompts customers to actually tell you yes.

An important rule to remember: *Price is never the way to create a wow experience*. The product is probably not a way to create a wow experience either, unless you are the *only* source for a particular product or service, which is unlikely. The wow moment occurs when you present the product, let customers know how it can solve their problems, and figure out how it makes them feel as well as how you present, service, and deliver that experience.

The best way to increase your customer base is to give clients more than their money's worth. Reducing price or cost does not add value or solve problems; it merely reduces the cost of the product and can actually *diminish* perceived value. Most salespeople think that price is a way to make a better deal or sell more products, but I can give you an almost endless list of companies that have gone out of business while operating as the lowest-cost provider. Because their margins are so low and they are forced to run so tightly, they don't bother to think in terms of wow and aren't able to financially deliver this kind of experience. Write down the names of at least three big companies that failed in the last 12 months because they offered the lowest price with no wow component. Some are among those same companies mentioned in Chapter 6 that have enormous advertising budgets and big promises of customer satisfaction. They added the fact that they were the lowest-priced provider to their pitch, but now they're out of business and unable to deliver *any* kind of service.

Look for every opportunity to go the extra mile and give that little bit of additional service; it can mean the difference between merely *satisfying* the client or customer and *dazzling* them. Just in the way you greet someone, answer the phone, or get them a cold drink can create the wow experience. When I was in my twenties, I was selling a highly competitive product. I was meeting with a prospect on a very hot day, so I asked him if he would like something to drink. He said, "I would love a Diet Coke." I left him and came back with a silver platter, one glass with ice and one without, straws in both, and a can of Diet Coke. As I pulled the tab and opened it for him, I smiled and asked, "How would you like it—in the can, a glass, or over ice?" The client looked at me and said, "Wow, nobody does that. You should be selling luxury yachts or something!" We made a deal on a highly competitive, high-margin product, and I closed the transaction without discounting the product. Even better, I continued to sell to this man and his family for years, and *they* all sent me business as well. They would bring people to me and tell their friends that regardless of what they paid me, I would exceed their expectations. Now *that* is advertising that works! There are unlimited creative ways to deliver a wow experience that have nothing to do with discounts or even the product being sold.

A friend of mine recently came to Los Angeles to take some courses that I had recommended. He was planning to stay at the Peninsula Hotel, where he normally stays. I suggested that he instead stay at the hotel where the course was being held. I admitted that the hotel I was recommending couldn't compete with the Peninsula in terms of location, proximity to shopping, or even the amenities to which he was accustomed, but I guaranteed that it would exceed the Peninsula's service and that he would get more out of his studies by staying there. He took my suggestion.

I called the hotel's managers and asked them to go the extra mile and do whatever it took to wow my friend. They welcomed him upon arrival; they unpacked his clothes, hung them in the closet, and made sure the staff addressed him by name each time they saw him in the lobby. How does an unknown, small hotel in a less-than-desirable location compete with—and even take customers away from—a great hotel in a prime location with an international name and all the amenities? By delivering wow experiences to customers who are so impressed that they refer others to it! You can't advertise wow; you can only deliver it.

The single best protection against a downturn in business is having an active list of wow-ed, elated, truly satisfied clients who give you a steady stream of continuing assignments because they *love* the way you treat them. You must also commit to wow the clients in your power base—whether they buy from you or not. Follow-up, contacts, e-mails, and personal visits are all opportunities to wow those on your list. Anyone can buy a product similar to yours, and someone is always willing to sell it for less. The only thing that keeps you above the fray is cultivating, nurturing, serving, and doing everything you can to amaze your current customers.

Don't seek to satisfy; seek to wow. *The more you wow, the less you have to promote—because others will do it for you!* If they give you a dollar, ask yourself, "How can I deliver 10 times that in terms of wow?"

Exercise

Delivering at "Wow" Levels

What are the two best ways to hold on to your clients?

1. _____
   _____
   _____

2. _____
   _____
   _____

Why is the wow experience even more effective when times are bad?

_____
_____
_____

What are three ways in which you can create a wow experience?

1. _____
   _____
   _____

2. _____
   _____
   _____

3. _____
   _____
   _____

CHAPTER
8

The Importance of Price

P rice is always a very sensitive issue, especially during times of economic contraction. You're constantly getting hammered with the notion that people don't have money, and your "weak" competitors are lowering price as a solution to a tougher environment. The reality is that money is tighter and people are scared and more selective with their purchases. The first response—an incorrect one—is to reduce price. A lower price won't necessarily sell your product or make up for the lost volume you may encounter. And I can assure you from experience that a lower price will not get your clients to buy your product if they aren't fully sold on its value, excited about it, and confident that it will solve their problems and/or make them happy.

Unless you are Wal-Mart or The Dollar Store, whose entire business models are built around very small margins and high controls on their inventories, the "lowest-price" approach will probably fail you. Selling on price is an indication of a weak-minded and poorly trained individual or organization. As I mentioned earlier, plenty of organizations that have used the lowest-price model have filed for bankruptcy or closed their doors this year alone.

If you are going to sell fewer products due to a tightened economy, you have to do a better job of determining your prospects' needs. You must then do a *great* job of building value and making your customers feel confident that your product will solve their problems in order to get the price you need to stay solvent.

Remember: Everyone is aware that things are tight. You have to make adjustments to respond to this knowledge, but lowering price shouldn't be one of them. A lower price might even convey a reduction in value to clients. People who are ready and willing to spend money during economic hardship are conditioned to believe that they can get a better deal—either because others are not buying or because your competitors are (incorrectly) using price to get their attention. Do the math, and you will discover that this lower-price-with-less-volume formula will not work out for you. You have to learn how to sell your product and justify the price by building value, selling yourself and your company, and creating a wow experience.

It is also important to understand that those who are ready to buy will not just shop your product against a competitor's like product; they're also comparing your product to unlike products. As they become more concerned about money, they become more selective about what they choose to purchase. So the question is what they will spend their money on. A lot of salespeople and managers miss this point; they only focus on what they sell without bothering to consider that their prospects may be contemplating completely unrelated investments. They become so concerned with direct competition that they overlook unrelated products and services that become competitive choices for the now more selective buyer.

An example of this might be the car dealer who is so worried about losing a deal to his direct competitor down the street that he shortcuts building value into the automobile. He discounts his price to compete with the other dealer down the street while the prospect decides to invest the $40,000 in a new kitchen for his home instead—all because the dealership failed to build real value. *During periods of contraction, the issue becomes* where *individuals direct their money*. Remember this rule: *Money will find what people perceive as value; not the lowest price*. If a prospect isn't completely convinced of the usefulness of your product or service, that person will elect to do something else with his or her money.

The value proposition is greatly misunderstood. Hopefully, the following example can clarify it for you. If I sell you a book for $30 and you give me $30, the reality is that you either believe that the book is worth more than $30, or you don't value your $30. You might feel like the book is worth $30, but because I didn't really convince you that it is worth more, you may decide that your money would be better invested in dinner with the family. People will not give you any amount of money if they think what they are getting is worth *exactly that much*. They will only do so when they believe that what they are getting is worth much more!

What does this have to do with selling in a changing economy and being able to advance and conquer? *Everything*. Periods of contraction require that you enhance value by taking the following specific steps.

- Do a better job of identifying what the buyer is trying to accomplish with your product. *"What is the number one thing you want this product to do for you or help you do?"*

- Demonstrate how your product's worth is greater than the price you are asking for it. Take the time to creatively build value that exceeds price and ensures that the prospect is making the right decision.

- Demonstrate how your product will sufficiently solve problems and why the customer will love it. People buy for two reasons: (1) to solve a problem; and (2) for love and to feel good. If they don't believe one of those two things, price will not matter. *"On a scale from 1 to 10, how would you rate this product?"*

- Be sure that the proposition you are presenting is within your customer's financial means. Having too much of a product is the fastest way of forcing you to cut your price.

- Become thoroughly versed in the fact that price is a myth—one that is disproven every day when people give up their money for something they desire. Check out my book, *Sell to Survive*, in which there is an entire chapter on this topic of the price myth, how it is a destructive belief, and how it is destructive to creating your own economy. You can find it at www.selltosurvive.com, or you can call my office at 1-800-368-5771.

Exercise

The Importance of Price

Price will not get you the business if you don't accomplish four other things first. What are they?

1. _____
   _____
   _____

2. _____
   _____
   _____

3. _____
   _____
   _____

4. _____
   _____
   _____

Why could lowering the price cause someone not to buy your product?

_____
_____
_____

(continued)

(continued)

What does competing with "unlike" products mean, and what are some examples?

_____

_____

_____

If I give you $100 for your product/service, what was it worth to me?

_____

_____

_____

Learn more about the price myth.

Visit www.grantcardone.com/resources

CHAPTER

9

Activate Second Sale to Boost Profits

One way to generate additional business is to maximize your first sales with add-ons or second sales. Though the second sale is actually easier to get than the first, 99.99 percent of all salespeople, managers, and companies miss this opportunity. You can spend hours and hours making the first sale but make a second sale (or add-on) in just a few minutes that will (1) be easier; (2) generate more profits; and (3) make your buyers even *more* satisfied with their purchases.

The problem is that most businesses and salespeople get so excited about the much-needed first sale that they are oblivious to and untrained in taking advantage of this additional opportunity. Because they lack proper training and erroneously believe that people buy on price, companies often do not attempt this second, easy sale. But your buyers will actually use ancillary purchases to support their first decisions; it's a phenomenon that's verified every day. Just visit Rodeo Drive in Beverly Hills. I dare you to find a person with only one bag in his or her arms. Or recall the last time you went to dinner and complained about the cost of that one special entrée you wanted to order. Yet once you agreed to reward yourself with that special entrée, you then continued to add other items. You asked to see the wine list, you splurged on an appetizer— you even ordered dessert. And you added all of these mere moments after fretting over the cost of the entrée.

No one is exempt from this inherently human tendency to spend additional money once the floodgates (or wallets) have been opened. People seem to use this second purchase to justify the earlier one. *You* can use this all-too-human habit to consummate the second sale by doing the following. Once the first sale is made, agreed upon, and closed—and after you have taken the time to congratulate the customer and acknowledge the purchase—suggest other possible add-ons to the first purchase. Even sensitive prospects who are on strict budgets will take you up on these second offers to justify their initial decision.

Again, make sure to suggest the additional service once the agreement has been made—not before. For instance, let's say that you sell advertising and that you've put together an advertising campaign for a client's company. Once you have made your presentation and proposal, agreed on price and terms, gone over the particulars, and closed the deal, congratulate the client and reiterate how helpful this program is going to be for him or her. Then suggest that the client increase the number of times he or she is going to run the ad or do a press release in addition to the initial ad. This second sale is easy, builds value for your client, and increases profits for your company.

Let's say you sell furniture and have made a living room sale that includes a sofa, two chairs, and a coffee table. Once you have solidified this sale and assured the purchaser that he or she will love it, say, "May I make a suggestion? This rug and lamp fit perfectly with what you are getting today and greatly complement the other furniture. I think they give the room an even more completed look. What do you think about adding them to your order?" Or, let's say you're selling clothes to a buyer who has agreed to purchase a suit, shirt, and tie. As you're ringing him up, you might want to say, "Congratulations. I know you are going to love these. May I suggest that you add this pair of shoes, a second tie, and these two shirts to keep this suit looking fresh all the time? It will allow you to create three outfits instead of just one." Wait for him to ask how much. Most of the time, you will get part or all of this second order. If he agrees, congratulations—you just made another sale without having to work with another customer! Double down and double up, as they say in Vegas.

Remember: Second money is easier to get than first money, and these add-on sales allow you to maximize the time, energy, and effort you've already put forth. You have increased your sales without increasing your customer count—something that's critical when there are fewer customers. This technique lets you increase the average dollar value of each project 25 to 40 percent or more with *virtually* no extra effort. I often look for ways to add ancillary assignments to the primary one. It's good for me, and good for my clients. I get more work, and they get a more complete service. Try it yourself. I promise that it works! Your goal is to advance and conquer, and that requires that you make the decision to maximize every opportunity to increase your business. This will not be a time to rely on the economy in which you live and work. This commitment requires action and creativity.

Exercise

Activate Second Sale to Boost Profits

What are three benefits of the second sale?

1. _____
   _____
   _____

2. _____
   _____
   _____

3. _____
   _____
   _____

What is the one thing on which you must have a firm grasp in order to pull off the second sale?

_____
_____
_____

What are the three things you must do before attempting the second sale?

1. _____
   _____
   _____

2. _____
   _____
   _____

3. _____
   _____
   _____

What are some examples of ways you can use this action?

_____
_____
_____
_____
_____

The Value-Added Proposition

During a recession, depression, business downturn, or soft economy it is probably not the appropriate time for you to increase your fees or prices—even if you feel you deserve it. You should probably defer any planned fee-increase announcements until later and instead keep your fees at their current levels during such a period. This is the time to make creative, value-added offers that further enhance how well your product is perceived. Obviously, you want to be sensitive to the market, use it to demonstrate this extra value, and encourage people to do business with you.

Note: You *are not* going to make an announcement to your customers and prospects that you are "holding the line" on prices due to the recession because of your desire to help them through this time. No one will do business with you because you showed sympathy for them. What you *will* do is add value to the same services that you have sold in the past by bringing extra attention to the things your product or service does. You need to get even *more* creative than you have before and strongly emphasize how you and your company are going to support, service, and stand behind your products, services, and proposals. This doesn't mean you give anything away nor should it be confused with using the second-sale strategy. However, it *does* mean that you'll need to highlight the other services that are included with your offer that don't cost the company or your client money. In addition to your product, you are going to offer what is referred to as value-added propositions, also known as unique selling propositions. A unique selling proposition is a real or perceived benefit of a good or service that differentiates it from the competing brands and gives buyers a logical reason to prefer your good or service over other brands.

So, maybe in addition to installing a product, you hold initial meetings for the entire group to whom you're selling, motivate and ensure buy-in from them, and conduct follow-up trainings after product installation. You can follow up further by holding teleconferences with clients throughout the year to continue to answer questions and make sure that they're familiarized with the new product. Though these unique selling propositions may be things you were willing to do last year, you *really* have to promote now in order to make your proposition appear unique. You don't reduce the price, but you do sweeten your proposal by building value.

In my experience, one of the reasons people stall when it comes to decision making is due to negative past experiences. The more unique you can make the proposition appear, the more success you will have in overcoming people's tendency to delay making a choice.

For example, I own apartment buildings, and when things tighten up, people shop more diligently. They want the most apartment for the least amount of rent. Because other apartment owners are feeling the pressure, they will start to reduce their rents, which puts downward pressure on my properties and their rental incomes. I don't want to be compared with the apartment building down the street and be forced to drop my price. Therefore, I look for creative ways to add value to my property so that we keep our occupancy high and don't erode our revenues. I distinguish myself from my competition by offering unique value-added options. When you start thinking of how to solve problems creatively—without lowering prices—you will come up with great propositions.

We did this exact exercise with one of our properties when our competition was lowering prices. Since we wanted to maintain income, we knew we would have to come up with something to differentiate our offering. We knew, for instance, that people love their animals and that many apartment complexes don't allow them. So we added fences to each of our downstairs units that allow our tenants to have dogs of any size. Because of this proposition, rents *and* occupancy at my building are now higher than at my competitors' properties, and I raised the overall value of the building by increasing my cash flow. Because I was creative and found distinctive ways to build value, my apartment product stands out from the rest of those in the marketplace.

Here's another example. Let's say that you own a salon and want to offer some kind of value-added proposition that makes it more attractive for people to spend money on getting their hair cut from you. You don't want to drop the price, though, since this will only remind them how tight money is and possibly keep them from coming to see you.

Instead, you call your clients and let them know about a new initiative:

"Hey, I wanted to call and tell you that we are now offering wine and cheese in my shop for anyone who comes in to get a haircut in the next two weeks. It's a lot of fun, and you're past due for a cut anyway, aren't you? We'll also be giving out free head and neck massages—so come on in for some relaxation time!" The cost of wine and cheese is almost nothing compared with the income you will generate from this creative value-added thinking. All you have to do is make the call, bring the wine and cheese from your house, and take an extra five minutes giving a head massage when you shampoo clients' hair.

Regardless of the type of business you run, you *must* build value, communicate that you are doing things differently by providing even more service, and highlighting how unique your proposal is. People want to feel good and receive special treatment, and they want to be told about what you're doing. There are endless ways in which you can add value without decreasing price and create more business for yourself and your company—even in a contracting marketplace. Selling is all about building value, so in order to create your own economy, you must become effective at selling. And to do any of this successfully, you must be completely sold on what you offer and have a complete commitment to your expansion—and a fierce disregard for contraction.

Remember: The value-added proposition should increase revenue without costing your company any additional money. Do not confuse this with the second sale or use any of your second-sale opportunities to make the unique value-added proposition. Now—more than at any other time—is when you promote and show excitement about your products, services, company, and yourself in a manner that adds value to each of these things and makes them unique in the market.

Exercise

The Value-Added Proposition

What are some obvious things you can include with your product or service that are value-added propositions that you have *not* done a good job of promoting?

_____

_____

_____

Write down two examples of companies or individuals that use value-added propositions in their offers.

1. _____

_____

_____

2. _____

_____

_____

(continued)

(*continued*)

Now write down three different ways you can create a value-added proposition without reducing price.

1. _____
   _____
   _____

2. _____
   _____
   _____

3. _____
   _____
   _____

Improve the Value-Add Proposition and increase sales.
Visit www.grantcardone.com/resources

11

Act Hungry

Now is the time to let your customers know you are hungry. It's *not* the time to act like you don't need their business. There is an old saying that tells people to *"fake it 'til you make it."* Well, this doesn't apply here! Instead, you want to *"act hungry to make sure you don't end up hungry."*

No one likes people who act like they are better than others or so important that they don't need your business. Everyone appreciates someone who goes the extra mile and really shows others that he or she wants, needs, and values others' business. You will never create a powerful, solvent, prosperous, and abundant economy with an attitude of arrogance. You better have your best game face on when economies tighten up; people who are looking for reasons *not* to do business with you won't tolerate any egotism. In almost every seminar I conduct, someone will say to me, "I'm afraid I might seem weak if I act like I want the business too much." My response is always the same: "The biggest mistake you can make is *not* to act like you're hungry for the business!" *You cannot afford to make mistakes in these times. Let your competitors act like they don't need the business, while you make it clear that you do.*

Let's face it: You need clients more than they need you in *any* economy, and just because you were a hotshot in the past means nothing now. I know companies, executives, and

115

individuals that are still acting like they're top in their industry because they used to be number one in their market, yet their current sales are off by 40 percent. Being number one doesn't pay bills—and your position is only as valuable as the degree to which you are profitable. What you did last year means nothing in the market today. History is laden with companies that were number one in their field but who only exist nowadays between the pages of books. Sears and Kmart are two perfect examples of these. Both dominated their fields at one time, but their arrogance cost them their positions—and now they're struggling in the market.

The primary goal in a shrinking economy is to close the gap in lost sales and keep finding creative ways to do so. There's no time to brag about your position or discuss yesterday's fortunes and successes. Spend all your time, energy, creativity, and resources in advancing your goals and getting so far ahead of the pack that you seize your competitors' business along the way. The real world of business is the most brutal battlefield in the world; it will not tolerate conceit or people who are living in the past. Customers don't value excuses, timing, reasons, ratings, yesterday, position; they only value results. If you want to create your own economy, you have to know what you are dealing with. The only way to impress the marketplace is to gain market share going forward—at which point, it will grant you all of its gold and treasures.

It's easy to act like you are invincible when you're busy, in demand, and have much more work than you can handle; however, it's not attractive. Knock off the arrogance and start acting hungry. Acting *hungry* means that you're aggressively ambitious or competitive. Perhaps it stems from a need to overcome poverty or past defeats or it is because your desire to succeed is so great. Regardless of your position in life, if you want to stay on top, you have to be willing to do *whatever it takes* to earn more business—during good times and bad.

You need to show great appreciation and gratitude for every opportunity you get. Be willing to bend over backward, sideways—even do handstands, if necessary—to let people know that you'll do whatever it takes to earn their business. Don't let yesterday's successes give you a false sense of security and make you feel like you don't need success today and tomorrow. *You must have your attention on the future to create one* and you *must* do things now that you didn't do before the slowdown.

If your market is down 40 percent and you are still operating with the same energy, effort, and actions that you did before the pullback, you are going to move backward—because your efforts have not adjusted to the reduction in business. Your absence of effort is likely due to a lack of awareness, an abundance of arrogance, or a combination of the two. So wake up and make the adjustments necessary to tweak your business to the economy's new realities. You absolutely must (1) make the mental adjustment that things are different and start acting accordingly; and (2) increase your activity. Just because you won the Super Bowl last year doesn't mean you don't go to spring camp and train next year. As any sailor knows, "yesterday's winds won't fill tomorrow's sails."

Always, always, always demonstrate your hunger and desire to grow your business by displaying how service oriented and interested you are in your clients on a daily basis. Follow up relentlessly and do *anything* you can (ethically and professionally, of course) in order to obtain someone's business—especially when things tighten. Be useful, courteous, accessible, humble, and now more than ever, willing to go the extra mile. Surpass any and all expectations, act like you really want someone's business—and do whatever you can to earn it.

Adjust your actions to match the reality of the situation; make sure potential clients know how much you *do* want their business. An attitude of "they need me more than I need them" always fails; treat your customers as though they're more valuable than you and your company—because they *are*. If you give your clients genuine reasons to like you, demonstrate an authentic willingness to do anything for them, are consistently helpful, and *never* quit, they will want to do business with you, whatever your business is.

Any time someone who serves me continues to exhibit that hungry desire to do anything humanly possible to earn my business, I find every reason possible to support him or her. I stick with that person as long as he or she keeps exhibiting that kind of hungry attitude, and I don't think I am unique this way. Most people want to be taken care of and paid attention to, and they crave this type of service from people because it is lacking in our culture. People wonder why their businesses fail in a country with countless citizens barely making it financially who are subject to the whims of the economy, dependent upon credit to pay their bills, and enslaved to someone else's economy.

If you want to expand and conquer and create a personal economy that allows you freedom and control, then make sure everyone knows how badly you want their business. Act like your life depends on every transaction, every moment of every day. And if you have to *tell* someone that you really want his or her business, well then, you probably aren't acting hungry enough!

Exercise

Act Hungry

Give an example of an instance in which you did business with someone who acted like he or she didn't need your business and how it made you feel.

_____

_____

_____

Give two examples of a time when someone bent over backward to earn your business.

1. _____

_____

_____

2. _____

_____

_____

(continued)

(*continued*)

Write three examples of ways you can demonstrate that you are hungry and willing to do anything to earn potential clients' business.

1. _____
   _____
   _____

2. _____
   _____
   _____

3. _____
   _____
   _____

Turn your hunger into a CLOSE.

Visit www.grantcardone.com/resources

CHAPTER

12

Expand Acceptable Client Profile

Most of the people with whom I work have a set of mental or written guidelines that determine which customers they desire and which they do not. While you may not even be conscious of these parameters, they can have a negative impact when things tighten. A depressed economy or personal business downturn requires that you relinquish any restrictions about your "ideal" or preferred customer. This isn't a time to be selective with your criteria; you may have to break some of your previous rules for those with whom you do business.

For instance, let's say you normally only have *Fortune* 500 companies as clients. You may want to consider taking on assignments from smaller firms as well since you need to adopt an appropriate game plan to ensure that you advance and conquer when things are tight. What you did yesterday may have worked then but probably won't be relevant today or tomorrow, so be willing to open up your client base to offset any pullback from your normal list. If your typical customer profile has diminished or clients have cut back on their budgets, you will be forced to look to wherever a flow of business could occur.

When economic conditions change, all of your earlier considerations and actions need to change along with them. The other day, I drove six hours round-trip to do a presentation for eight people—something that wouldn't have been practical for me to do a year ago. Whether it was worth it or not is to be determined, but when things tighten, I immediately loosen up any and all earlier restrictions. I need to get in front of more clients, and I know I have to go the extra mile to offset the reduction.

Now is the time to be prepared to change past decisions in order to achieve your goal of advancing and conquering. It's not the time to hold on to any beliefs from the past that will keep you from moving forward.

Let's say, for example, that you are an accounting firm that has traditionally only worked on major annual reports. Now you might want to consider doing smaller quarterly reports—without your normal annual agreement—in order to generate some much-needed revenue. Maybe you expand your client profile to include smaller companies as well. This doesn't mean you throw your standards out the window and work for anyone who calls you; you're simply readjusting your acceptable criteria during this temporary lull in order to accommodate a wider range of prospects and projects.

How far should you take this? It's up to you. If, for example, you normally have a minimum project fee of $1,000, you might accept $500 assignments, but you probably would not take on $50 assignments. When you think about it, there are probably a lot of things you do for free everyday anyway. While the initial presentation you make prior to earning someone's business costs *you* money, it's usually free to that person, and you may or may not get the business. I always remain open to creating new relationships in order to establish new contacts that may one day become regular clients.

So get real during economic contractions, and know that you will have to make adjustments in the way you think, the people with whom you're willing to work, and how you conduct business. You may not even be aware of some of the things that are holding you back—so you may have to do some digging. Ask yourself why you don't do business in a particular zip code area or with a certain sized client or group? Start looking for new markets and clients, and spend your energy and resources to determine what you have to do to go get them. You may uncover some hidden consideration or agreement not to approach that sector, or maybe you just didn't have time for it before.

Forget yesterday and keep all your attention on what you're going to do to create a new tomorrow. Reassessing your list of potential clients should be an operating basis at *all* times, but it's even more critical now. Remember to be hungry and that no one likes arrogance. You need clients, relationships, business flow, action, new relationships, and new business. You need to adjust for any loss in opportunities and revenue due to the constraints on the marketplace. These new considerations—and your willingness to work with a broader range of people—may cause you to find yourself opening up to opportunities you've never imagined before, expanding your power base, and finding sales and clients that you might have missed, denied, or overlooked during better times.

Exercise

Expand Acceptable Client Profile

Why would you want to open up restrictions on those with whom you consider doing business during contractions?

_____

_____

_____

Write down a list of clients with whom you have previously preferred not to work because of spoken or unspoken agreements.

_____

_____

_____

Make a list of clients with whom you would be willing to work now in order to put this action into place.

_____

_____

_____

Effective Marketing Campaigns

One of the first things individuals and businesses do during periods of contraction is reduce their advertising and marketing. *Big* mistake. Now is the time to hammer your business into the marketplace with cost-effective marketing plans that let the world know who you are, what you do, and what you have to offer. Despite your tendency to want to save money in any way possible, now is *not* the time to retreat. Let your competitors' contract to the point that they no longer exist while you press your bet, and if you are going down, go down swinging.

It's especially important now to be at the fore in your clients'—and potential clients'—minds. While this expand-and-conquer action is completely counterintuitive to all the bad news, you must effectively and aggressively market yourself and your business if you are going to survive, prosper, and capture market share from your competitors.

Obviously, you want to be smart about this tactic and avoid spending money on strategies that don't work. When things get slow, increase the amount of time you spend on marketing and prospecting for new business. You're usually able to get the best price for traditional advertising and marketing campaigns during slowdowns since other people are doing *less* advertising. In addition to traditional approaches, research and employ creative ways to make your organization more widely known within the circles and communities in which you sell. For instance, if you usually devote 10 percent of your time and energy to marketing and prospecting when things are fairly busy, you might increase this to 50 percent when things are slow.

As we've discussed previously, a lull in business requires that you expend extra effort to attract clients, follow up on leads, and stay in contact with and extend your power base. While you can accomplish this through traditional advertising, you can also utilize some activities that don't cost any money: phone calls, personal visits, mail, e-mails, fliers, social networking on the Internet, church activities, newsletters, seminars, briefings, "good news" newsletters, instructional videos, community involvement, magazine writing, taking on a public office, speaking at rotary clubs, coaching your kid's soccer team—and so on. Most if not all of these methods are fairly original, build tremendous goodwill, get you better known, and cost nothing but your time and energy!

The second part of this approach dictates that whatever you do, be sure you stick with it. Take action consistently and aggressively during every day, week, and month and throughout the year. You must commit to a marketing program throughout the year—not just when you need the business—in order for any one of these initiatives to work. Whether it's a traditional advertisement or some of the other, more innovative marketing strategies already mentioned, make sure you can stay with it because *all* marketing takes some time to get traction. When planning a public relations or advertising campaign, I look at how much it will cost to run that program over the course of a year, not a week or month. While this technique ensures a steady stream of new business contacts in the future, it isn't guaranteed to reap immediate results. The promotion you conduct today sets in motion a selling cycle that will result in new business when you need it six months into the future.

It is just as important that this campaign enhance your reputation throughout the community or circles in which your product is needed. In addition, the fact that you are out there doing something about your business—instead of just sitting idly at your desk, waiting for things to turn around—will give you added confidence.

The types of marketing that work best in an economic contraction—and during all economies, since they are most effective—are a combination of results-oriented direct marketing (direct-response print ads, sales letters, self-mailers, special offers) and low-cost or no-cost visibility-enhancing publicity techniques (press releases, articles, speeches, booklets, seminars, newsletters, radio and TV interviews). For instance, my company offers free seminars. I do at least 25 of these per year to introduce people to my company, ideas, products, and services in order to continue to expand my future possibilities. Yes, it costs time and energy, but *not* doing these things risks the company's future. Don't think of marketing in terms of just costing money since a lot of efforts can be made without any budget just by utilizing your energy. For example, over the course of one week, I personally did 15 radio interviews, met with a group of businesspeople who were located three hours from my office, had two free post-seminar private-speaking engagements, sent out 50 books with a personal note to business owners around the country, and wrote and mailed a combination newsletter–video e-mail to contacts in my entire database.

Attack every aspect of your marketing platform with massive action and energy. *Massive* is defined in the dictionary as "large in comparison with what is typical." My own personal definition is "that amount of action that will create new problems for yourself and your company."

Yes, you read that right. You want to *create* new problems. Most people stop short of this approach; in fact, they usually try to avoid *all* problems, just to end up with the same old boring recurring situations that they have had for years. People don't advance and conquer because they don't take enough action or follow this up with *more* massive action. They then end up with dull, familiar problems instead of adventurous and positive problems. *Massive* is critical to making your marketing efforts effective.

Never try to replace the more labor-intensive marketing efforts mentioned earlier with traditional paid advertising. And never assume that just because you don't own a company that you don't need to advertise and market *yourself*. The goal is to advance and conquer, not just be along for whatever ride the economy provides. Increase your responsibility to change your conditions by doing more marketing for yourself, independent of the company.

One of the reasons people become so insecure when unemployment goes up during a period of contraction is because they become aware that they are at risk. You have to aggressively and effectively learn to market yourself, or you will experience downturns in your business—even during thriving economic conditions. It is a misconception today among salespeople and employees that the company should do the advertising and marketing and those who work there should *just* collect paychecks. This line of thinking renders the individual more dependent upon the company, leaving him or her more intensely affected by whatever the business experiences. That person ultimately becomes a slave, with no control over his or her own economy. Individuals should be treated and conduct themselves like a business within the business, with the intent of creating their own economies that run because of their own production.

Regardless of your position, you must effectively market yourself as an individual to make yourself more valuable to your company, its clients, and the marketplace. You want to be invulnerable to the downturn. When markets contract, jobs do too, and those who appear the least valuable to the business are the ones who are let go first. Even good, loyal workers lose jobs during tough times—not because they didn't do a good job or weren't loyal to the organization. It is usually due to the fact that they did not do a good enough job of marketing themselves as too valuable to be terminated. So make sure that you present yourself as one of the irreplaceable members of your company.

Increase your value to the business and its clients and in the marketplace and you will never lose your job, no matter how significant economic problems become.

It is certainly not my intention to offend anyone in regard to this very sensitive issue. However, when I hear that someone has lost his or her job of 20 years with a company that didn't close its doors, well, that person must realize that someone made a decision to let go of him or her instead of someone else. During my first job out of college, middle management attempted to fire me on at least six occasions because—as they so eloquently stated—"Grant is difficult to manage and causes problems." Yet each time, upper management overturned middle management's decision because I was doing such a good job of marketing to my customers and selling the company's products. Executive management was not willing to risk losing the relationships I had created or the business I generated. On one occasion, upper management laid off my manager instead because the organization perceived me as being more valuable than him. In hindsight, I do agree that I was unnecessarily difficult to manage at that time, but my production levels were so high compared with those of others that it made me almost invincible. (I added *almost* in there to feign some humility.) Nothing will provide you with more protection than the ability to generate revenue—something that's done by taking massive action, effectively marketing, staying in front of customers, and getting the job done!

Unless you or your family owns the business (and sometimes, even if your family *does*), the only way you are going to ensure your own success is to outproduce everyone else. Your career's future should *never* be left up to a manager, the company, or the economy; it must always depend on your ability to get into the marketplace, effectively promote yourself, establish and cultivate relationships, inform people of who you are and what you do, and then turn those contacts into contracts. Do that, and you will never be without work or money. You will advance and conquer accordingly. Remember: Effective marketing is about more than merely spending money to advertise. It's about *investing* energy to make yourself known and valuable throughout the market.

Exercise

Effective Marketing Campaigns

Why is it an oft-made mistake to reduce advertising and marketing during contractions?

_____

_____

_____

How does marketing and advertising apply to you, regardless of your position?

_____

_____

_____

(continued)

(*continued*)

What are some traditional ways to advertise yourself and your company in your marketplace?

_____

_____

_____

What are some more creative, less traditional approaches to marketing yourself that cost energy but not money?

_____

_____

_____

Learn new ways to market yourself.

Visit www.grantcardone.com/resources

14

Repackaging for Increased Profits

When you're cranking out business at record speeds, you miss opportunities with your products that become incredibly obvious during tough economic or competitive times. When budgets tighten up, some companies and/or individuals may no longer have the budgets to afford your products as they're packaged—or the company size to justify purchasing them. It's also likely that while they might still be able to afford your product, the hysteria that accompanies economic contractions has incited a fear of spending money. Since they are now much more selective about their purchases, they're unlikely to buy your offering unless it is repackaged to accommodate their new financial parameters.

There are two things in which people lack confidence that are exaggerated during contractions: (1) the ability to make good decisions; and (2) the ability to create more money. While you can't handle every fear and insecurity your buyer has, it may be worth your while to look for ways to repackage your merchandise when things slow down. This allows you to accommodate smaller clients and reduced budgets and increase your value proposition.

For instance, when competitors start moving in on my territory or a downturn occurs, I immediately assess my product line for ways to repackage and proactively accommodate the change in people's thinking and budgets.

Despite new limits on my clients' resources, I want to express that it still makes sense for them to continue to do business with me. Advance and conquer; don't retreat and contract. Find creative ways to keep flowing with the changes in the market. For instance, I might rebundle a $500 product into ten $50 purchases or repackage the payment plan into three installments of $170 each. When you're committed to introducing people to your products, maintaining your client base, making progress, and keeping people connected to what you do, you *will* come up with innovative solutions. Just keep creating, move forward, and keep your eyes open for all kinds of solutions. Your competitors are liable to surrender market to you if you continue to outwit them.

Another example: My company runs a school in Orlando to which clients send their management teams for four days of training. When I'm looking for ways to repackage our products, I think of clients who may be wary about the cost of flights and hotels. So before my clients can even verbalize concern, I consider ways to handle possible future objections. In this case, we were prompted to promote our school as an inclusion to our seminar and other products. We merely increased the price of our seminars, and included the cost of the school, flights, and hotel. Remember, during tight times it is not true that people invest money in the lowest-priced solution but are much more careful about what solutions they invest in. This form of bundling or repackaging introduced our school to people who might not have otherwise attended. These attendees then return to their companies and recommend our program to others in the organization and we experience a surge in business when others are crying.

We then tried to figure out how to present our product in a way that resolved all the cost issues in the customer's mind and would actually provide them with greater solutions and increased value. We realize during times of economic contraction clients are much more selective in how they invest their resources in the new economic reality. This desire to address our customers' current financial budget concerns prompted us to design an incredible and revolutionary never-before-used sales training virtual technology product that can be found at www.virtualsalestraining.com. This new virtual and interactive tool born out of the creative commitment to resolve customer budget concerns allows our existing customers and new customers to access me 24 hours a day, 7 days a week. With just the click of a button, I am able to run daily sales meetings for the company, provide complete training for the entire organization, provide full testing and certification, provide total accountability to management, and literally be a personal coach for every salesperson and manager in the organization no matter how big. And I am able to do that without anyone spending money on travel and hotels or more importantly never missing a client opportunity. The moment we introduced our virtual program it exploded into the market with incredible results. We not only reactivated our current clients with a whole new product offer but we have since attained clients that we were never able to attract in the past.

While this program doesn't replace our school by any means or live engagements, it does supplement our core products and even drives more people to our schools, seminars, and other offerings. All the client needs in order to take advantage of this initiative is a computer. Clients can train their staff to handle every sales situation as well as access expert advice on increasing production in real time anytime they choose. Entire sales organizations are going online to use our Quick Close technology, which allows me to assist them in closing a deal while they are actually involved in the transaction. The user identifies a problem or situation and I pop up on his or her computer and give advice on how I'd approach a similar situation. A virtually "live" training session—with no boarding pass necessary!

The problem the client was faced with during the economic contraction of finding training with reduced budgets, forced us to look at new solutions and create an entirely new product line! This action of repackaging opened us up to creating a revolutionary product line, one that not only expanded our business but literally is changing the way people train, motivate, and improve sales performance. Without the quandary the contraction introduced, we may have rested on our laurels—and never even imagined designing this product. Remember, repackaging to solve problems didn't just satisfy our existing clients; it allowed us to attract brand new customers and reenergized the company during a time when energy is everything!

Let's say, for example, that you sell advertising and that you have a customer who currently can't afford for you to write a $5,000 direct-mail package. However, he *can* afford to pay you $500 to critique a package he writes himself. Or maybe you're a consultant with a client who can no longer justify spending $100 an hour for your services. You might design an alternative offering that provides your client with teleconferences and/or videoconferencing instead. Maybe now is the time to get your client's staff to work on newsletters to your clients. Maybe it's time to write your first book that you have wanted to write for years. Even if you don't get it on the bookshelves, you can get it to your clients to show them you are still in the game and still expanding. If your clients aren't spending money with you now because of monetary restrictions, repackaging to provide them with new solutions will keep you connected to them, reenergize the troops, give you new reasons to stay in contact—and when you come up with the right solution it will bring in much-needed revenue.

Freelancers, consultants, and other service providers can repurpose their expertise and services in a variety of formats: hourly and/or telephone consultations, critiques, newsletters, special reports, booklets, audio tapes, instruction manuals, books, seminars, blogs, advice columns, etc. Manufacturers and other product sellers can offer compact models, economy sizes, no-frills versions, special discounts, payment plans, and smaller minimum orders. For example, automobile giant General Motors is now introducing a 60-day money back guarantee—something the company never even considered to be an option before. The goal is to eliminate fear of decision making or loss from the customer's mind-set in order to encourage more buyers. Those of you who have seen your core product's sales drop off may want to increase your focus on servicing already-sold products. Service sales typically increase when overall sales diminish during difficult financial times since people often decide that it's more economically sound to fix or improve what they already own rather than replace it.

These alternative reassembled products or services may not provide as complete a solution as your earlier offers did. You shouldn't see them as a compromise, but rather a way to continue to accommodate your clients. Again, arrogance has no place during periods of contraction; the market is changing, and you must change along with it. Failing to offer an adjusted version of your merchandise might well mean a potential loss to a competitor who is willing to do so. If you don't offer it, someone else probably will, at which point, you will have compromised everything by refusing to be flexible to economic fluctuations.

Finding new, smaller clients who might be interested in your revised products is another option—and a much better solution than losing the business entirely. When the big companies are not giving you large orders at high prices, selling these alternatives to the less affluent or budget-minded segment of the market can put lots of extra dollars in your pocket, maintain much-needed cash flow, and keep you in front of your audience. And realize that repackaging doesn't always mean smaller sales. In fact, one of our product lines actually doubled in gross revenue because we repackaged it in a way that included services of very little cost to us. However, it doubled the value proposition and the product's closing effectiveness during a time when our competitors were getting their heads handed to them.

Once you have repackaged, you may discover completely fresh product lines to get excited about, along with a new story to bring to your clients. This excitement is critical to advancing in *any* economic climate, especially during times of contraction. Take the time to creatively repackage. I assure you that this will elicit new products, solutions, and opportunities that you would not have otherwise discovered.

Exercise

Repackaging for Increased Profits

What are the two things in which people lack confidence that are exaggerated during contractions?

1. _____

   _____

   _____

2. _____

   _____

   _____

(continued)

(*continued*)

What are two client situations that are addressed with repackaging?

1. _____
_____
_____

2. _____
_____
_____

What are five ways to repackage your products or services?

1. _____
_____
_____

2. _____
_____
_____

3. _____
_____
_____

4. _____
_____
_____

5. _____
_____
_____

The Power Schedule to Advance and Conquer

It is critical during a slow period that you keep a very tight, disciplined schedule—something I call a *power schedule*—to keep yourself and your company focused and productive. It's fairly easy to become immobilized by bad news and find yourself doing little more than being worried, scared, and unproductive. But when things tighten up, you must be *more* disciplined, structured, and constructive with the time you have—not less. *Any production, output, effort, or action done in sufficient quantities on a regular basis is better than no production—and it will get you results.* Don't just think of an economy in terms of money but of all the elements that compose it—goods, services, goodwill, clients, resources, equipment, activity, contact, and any efforts at production. The word *production* comes from the word *produce*, which means to cause to have existence or to happen or bring about. It also means to compose, create, or bring out by intellectual or physical effort. If you want to cause something to have existence, you must combine time with actions to produce the economy you desire. Consider this simple formula:

$$\text{Time} \times \text{Actions} = \text{Measure of Advance}$$

The degree to which you advance is only limited by the amount of time and action you invest. While much—if not most—of the world vehemently refuses to spend time on activities that won't immediately pay off, I would personally rather be productive and not be paid than not be productive and not be paid. In other words, I would rather do *something* for free than nothing at all. While many might disagree with this perspective, I can assure you that sooner or later, the productive person will be paid in some way, and inefficient people won't. To put it a different way: *The person who willingly swings the bat has a better chance at success than the person who refuses to swing. Any* efforts—even poorly executed ones—will aid your progress toward advancing and conquering, especially if you make them regularly and follow them up with subsequent action. It's especially important during a period of contraction to develop a disciplined commitment to using your time and energy. Most people don't have enough of the "advance" component in their daily schedules. If you want to move yourself forward, you have to do a lot, and you have to do a lot consistently.

Get your head around the idea that any action is better than none and that the more action you take, the more solvent your economy will become. Then pack your calendar with efforts at production. You should increase activity at least to the degree that the economy has contracted (bear in mind, this formula does not apply in reverse). Time is indeed money here, and the way in which you utilize your time today will determine how much money you have tomorrow. You have to consider the long term at all times; there are no quick fixes.

There seem to be a lot of people who aren't willing to expend energy without complete assurance of (usually immediate or short-term) payoff. An attitude like this only guarantees the demise of your economy. I then see others setting conditions on what they are willing to do and hear others say, "There is no way I am going to work any harder than I have been" or "There is no way I will work for that little bit of money." Abandon this kind of outlook at once. You have to be *willing* to do whatever it takes, regardless of how much effort it takes or how insignificant the payoff seems to be. If I had to take a second job flipping hamburgers to take care of my family, I would flip burgers. If I have to wash cars to take care of my family, I will wash cars. Drop the arrogance, your old beliefs, and any limitations on what you are willing to do, and get going on producing your economy.

One of the most difficult things to do during tough economic periods is to keep your mental state and outlook positive and focus on spending your time wisely. Pessimistic thinking, a negative attitude, and the tendency to cling to old ideas can function as a cancer that destroys any chance of an improved future. When things become especially grueling, it's that much more vital to make the most of every moment you have and be mindful of the positive. Consider the phrase I used before: "Time is money." During economic contractions, business slows down so you should have more time. If business is off 20 percent, you should have 20 percent more time! Time actually expands during contractions, now the question is what will you do with more time. The way you choose to schedule this "extra" time determines how well you'll weather the storm compared with others. Everyone has basically the same amount of time available, but the most industrious people do a better job of making the most of it.

Beginning each day on a disciplined schedule that keeps you busy and is filled with worthy actions is critical to keeping you focused on solutions. While the items on your calendar do not all have to be business related, they should all beget production of some sort. This could and should include spiritual, personal, and physical development; improving relationships with family, friends, and colleagues; volunteering; training; education; and the like. Starting each day with a workout and finding time to study are vital ways to make "downtime" more effective. I often say the following in my seminars: *"The more you produce, the more you can produce!"* Increasing your efforts in virtually any facet of your life will lead to enhanced performance in other seemingly disconnected areas. But without a plan or commitment to using time productively, you won't be able to generate enough with the time you have.

When things at your company were moving along well, you probably claimed that you didn't have time to exercise, study, or get involved with community affairs. Well, now you have the time. Even as a write this, I am reminded of other times in my life when things were not going well for me, and I implemented the use of this disciplined schedule strategy to get my head out of my backside. I increased my level of production in any area in order to get some momentum and get myself out of the hole I had dug for myself. Anytime I get into a period of low levels of production—a "funk," as some call it—I tighten my schedule and get a bit more rigid about how I use my time.

The first thing I decide when committing to my schedule is what time I will go to sleep and what time I will wake. If you don't control what time you go down, you will never be able to manage what time you wake up. Though we all have alarm clocks to get us out of bed in the morning, we usually lack a commitment to a strict bedtime. But establishing one helps us wake up feeling rested, focused, and prepared to produce. Sleep becomes the pivotal part of my work schedule; it provides the rejuvenation and energy I need to maximize the hours I am awake. Once you confirm your sleeping and waking times, you can then *pack* the rest of your day with production-oriented endeavors that add to your economy's expansion, make you feel good about yourself, increase your understanding, enhance your attitude, and create opportunities for new income.

These activities might include making direct contact with clients and potential clients; sending out mailers and promotional material; marketing, planning, and surveying for clients; repackaging products; scheduling personal visits; making calls; cleaning files; conducting quality checks on services; redesigning slide presentations; working out; investing in study time; writing a book; eating healthy; rebuilding your Web site; and anything else you can imagine. Commit yourself to a schedule and include those activities that bring you personal pleasure, keep you busy moving forward, and are heavily focused on accessing opportunities. This last element is important; otherwise, you may find yourself engaging only in pastimes with which you are comfortable but that probably won't produce revenue. For instance, most people take lunch every day of the week. That one hour is not the time to organize files or plan a marketing campaign, but it's the perfect opportunity to take a client to lunch.

Next, figure out what percentage of your schedule puts you in front of people who can either purchase your products and services or activate others who may be able to do so. I would personally want to be in front of prospective clients more than 50 percent of the time. You may have to rework your schedule to hit your desired proportion. Don't just plan busy time to have "something" to do; stay occupied with things that help you advance and conquer.

Once your power schedule is balanced, follow it and stay true to it! This is going to be a fun exercise in controlling your own time. For instance, if you've set lunch from noon to 1:00, then let everyone know that you have a packed day and must leave promptly at 1:00. Then move directly to the next activity on your schedule. If you have a marketing meeting with colleagues scheduled for 2:15, tell them exactly how much time you have for that meeting—and stick to it. You will give yourself and others the impression that you are busy, and because you put time limits on each meeting, you will find yourself getting more done in less time.

Now is the time to do *more* while others are doing less. Expand while others contract. Conquer while others retreat and surrender. There are hundreds of things that you have neglected over the years that you now have the time to do. You don't do things like sleep, watch TV, complain, take long lunches and dinners, gossip, read newspapers, worry, or waste time because you are lazy. These behaviors are simply the result of a lack of commitment to a power schedule. When you have other places you have to be and don't have time for these things, then you just don't do them.

Make it clear to the world every day that you have "things to do and people to see." Adopt this as your mantra so you can stay above the fray, free from the barrage of negativity, thereby ensuring the expansion of your bright and prosperous economy. Move fast—heck, even run—from one activity to the next. Increase your frequency, speed, vibration, and activities. Travel as though you have someplace important to go and something important to do, and both will come to fruition. Take this opportunity to gain control and make the most of your time. Use it to catch up on all the things that will make you more valuable to yourself and others.

There are so many possibilities of items to put on your power schedule that will advance your new economy. Take on another job, learn a new skill, improve those you have in some way, start a home business, get involved with a direct-marketing opportunity, help solve the problems in the marketplace, or join a group of people with common interests. You can learn a new language, learn more about the Internet, read a book each week, listen to audio programs, help out with the community, run for office, help out your church—the possibilities are endless.

Most people use time as an excuse for not doing things that they know will be good for them and claim that they just don't have time. But the reality is that most of these people simply refuse to put worthwhile items on their schedule. Again, we all have the same amount of time. Treat yours like it is valuable. Make sure you max out every moment of every day, and I promise, you will feel better about yourself, and better things will happen to you.

If you operate this way during a downturn, you will already have momentum when things turn around because you will have honed the discipline, skills, education, connections, and muscle that others didn't. When people ask, "Why is he always moving so fast?" my answer is, "That's how I roll." When they ask, "What's the hurry? Chill out," inspire them by saying, "The more I do, the more I can do, and the more I can do, the more I get done!" When they tell you, "Slow down and enjoy your life," tell them, "I can't slow down. I have an economy to create so that I can ensure the future of my family." Be careful of people who challenge your desire to get more done, as they are dangerous to themselves and others.

In addition to creating your new power schedule, make a list of *all wasteful actions* in which you are currently involved. This action is so very important that I actually could have made it a chapter on its own. Write down all the things you do that *in no way* can possibly contribute to future production or enhance the way you feel about yourself.

Once you have your list of wasteful activities, decide where on your new schedule these belong. I am not suggesting you get rid of all of them, but at least limit the amount of time you spend on them. I confess that I myself play Xbox occasionally. While I'm aware that it doesn't contribute to my production in any way, I enjoy playing it. I don't cut it out completely, but I do restrict it so that it doesn't cross over into my production time. In this way, I am not deprived of my playtime.

Now, start creating your new schedule. Write down what time you go to sleep tonight and what time you will wake up tomorrow. Here are a couple of tricks for those of you who love to sleep: Disable the snooze button on your alarm clock and keep the shades open on your windows where you sleep so that when the sun rises, it makes it difficult for you to stay in bed. Once bedtime and wake time are penciled in, then start filling in the rest of the day. The next items to add are breakfast, lunch, and dinner, so include those times. Now, continue to fill in the rest of the day with those things that you want to accomplish. Remember, most people get less done than they want—not because they are lazy but because they don't have a schedule. For instance, the first thing I do when I wake up in the morning is write down my life goals. I do this again before I go to sleep at night, so I have both of these actions on my schedule. After writing my goals, I have a 20- to 30-minute workout, followed by a healthy breakfast.

Construct the rest of your schedule, packing in every bit of the day with a planned event or action. When asked, "Do you operate your life exactly by the schedule?" my answer is, "Of course not." But each day, I am able to look at what I am committed to accomplishing. I would rather have a full schedule and wonder how I'm going to get all this done than have no schedule and become apathetic because there is nothing to do. Regardless of the economy, I commit each day to something that moves me into the market. The more I have on my schedule, the better chance I have of doing something productive. The more I get done, the better I feel—and the better I feel, the more I get done. When you feel better and actually start getting more done each day, you will find yourself rewarded in the marketplace for activities that had nothing to do with your job.

Here's an example of a recent day's schedule:

6:00	Wake up, drink water with lemon, write down my goals
6:15–7:00	Work out, listen to training material, swim and shower
7:00	Eat breakfast with family
7:20–8:00	Drive to office, pay a personal visit to client. Use all driving time to listen to training material.
8:00–8:15	Meet with group
8:16–9:00	Write weekly article for *Huffington Post* and *Business News*
9:00–10:00	Attend meeting to plan Web site strategy, promotion, and marketing
10:00–11:50	Direct client calls, followed up with mail and e-mail
12:00–2:00	Lunch with VIP client

2:00–3:00	More writing on book/product development meetings
3:00–4:30	Create new PowerPoint for latest seminar
4:30–5:00	Personal client—drop in on my way home
5:15–6:30	Downtime—play and family
6:30–8:00	Continue writing a new book/do research for an upcoming radio show regarding the economy
8:00–10:00	Watch recorded movie with family (avoiding news)
10:00	Shower, write goals, spend time with my wife, get to bed

---

Exercise

The Power Schedule to Advance and Conquer

What are two things that a very tight, disciplined schedule can get you?

1. _____

_____

_____

2. _____

_____

_____

(continued)

(*continued*)

Why is any production better than no production?

_____

_____

_____

What are some things you have neglected doing?

_____

_____

_____

What are some wasteful actions in which you are involved each day?

_____

_____

_____

What are the first two things to which you should commit when creating a schedule?

1. _____

_____

_____

2. _____

_____

_____

Create a schedule right now for the rest of the day and the week and stick to it as closely as possible.

_____

_____

_____

16

An Advance-and-Conquer Attitude

As discussed in the previous chapter, your attitude is going to determine how much action you take and how effective it is. It's always a challenge to remain positive—even more so during economic setbacks. This is the case for you, your customers, and all those with whom you compete. The person who can maintain an optimistic outlook when things are tough will have a significant advantage and a better chance at advancing and conquering.

The most dangerous component of a slowdown isn't usually the reality of the economic factors; it's the amount of damaging thinking that can infiltrate the marketplace as well as affect the individuals who support and spread such thinking. While bad attitudes never show up on a profit-and-loss statement, they *always* have something to do with the bottom line.

It's best during these times to avoid negativity—and the hopelessness, lack of confidence and direction, and depression it causes—at all costs. All of these factors will start to manifest themselves in your actions and results. Prospects and clients will sense any pessimism on your part and will interpret your actions as those done out of desperation or worry. This will most likely prompt them to respond to your proposals out of fear, which is never good for you.

Countless surveys have demonstrated proof that negativity can actually contribute to poor health, accidents, and lower levels of production. The American Medical Association even believes that 90 percent of illnesses are psychosomatic, or caused by the mind. If you believe that you will get sick, you have a better chance of getting sick. If you believe you will get in a car wreck, you'd better call the body shop—because you'll soon have to get your car repaired. If you don't think there is anything you can do during times of contraction, you'll support this belief by actually doing less. This self-fulfilling prophecy shows the power of your mind and attitude.

A man named Sangeeta Iyer conducted research that validated this theory and wrote about it in an article titled "Healing Is Believing: The Placebo Effect." This is an excerpt:

> Placebo is any treatment that is devoid of specific actions on the patient's symptoms or diseases that, somehow, can cause an effect upon that patient. A placebo can be a "sugar-pill"; or fake surgery/therapy can even be effective. In recent years, the effect of the placebo is becoming as great as that of a given medication.
>
> A person's beliefs and hopes about a treatment, combined with their gullibility, seem to have a significant biochemical effect. Positive results from a placebo are being noticed in patients being treated for a variety of disorders from depression.

At this point, the more cynical reader will ask, "Grant, are you saying I should just believe things are good when they really are not—and then everything is going to turn out good?" The answer is yes, I *would* suggest that you have a better chance at success if you fool yourself into thinking that things *will* improve—and that you can have a hand in improving them.

Reality is an interesting element to decision making because it seems to change drastically depending on whom you are talking to. Ask three different people how they feel about today's weather (let's say, 85 degrees and sunny), and you will probably get three different responses: (1) It's great! I love the summer; (2) It's terrible. I'm sweltering in this suit; and (3) It doesn't matter much to me. All three are the truth for the individual expressing them, and each response will influence the outcome of that person's day. So it's merely a question of how you see a situation—and occasionally convincing yourself that you can change the outcome.

At some time or another over the course of your career, you will experience business cycles during which things slow down. Your clients hear the same negative news you do, and bad news never fuels positive outcomes. They don't want more negativity; they can get that free at home from their TV in seemingly unending amounts. They don't want to see it on your face or in your actions, responses, or attitude. Act competent, exude success, and be positive and optimistic regardless of what is happening around you. Potential customers will be much more attracted to—or at least intrigued by—positive people. I was cohosting my regular weekly radio show in Los Angeles, talking about the importance of being positive in getting a job when unemployment rates are soaring. A caller texted the radio station saying, "That guy Cardone is obnoxious." I responded by saying,

"The guy who finds me obnoxious probably really admires and loves me, and that is his way of saying it." I wasn't being arrogant—I was looking for the positive. A woman I wanted to date years ago said the same thing about me—and she just delivered my first child! She simply couldn't resist my positive attitude, relentless follow-up, unwillingness to take no for an answer, and commitment to continue to show her attention—even after she had labeled me obnoxious.

I have endured several serious recessions as an active member of the business world, and sooner or later, they all end. None of them will last forever, and the way you handle yourself during that time has more to do with your current and future situation than the economy itself. Your attitude affects everyone around you—those at home, at work, and everywhere in between. I want my wife, daughter, four dogs, employees, colleagues, clients, and friends to see me as someone who instills hope and a positive attitude, *especially* when things are challenging.

I would suggest that everyone reading this immediately adopt a kind of program that focuses on positive thinking and offers constructive solutions. The positive attitude you need to succeed in business is not on CNN, CNBC, FOX, MSNBC, ABC, NBC, CBS, or any of the other cable or radio channels or any newspaper printed in the United States of America. In fact, the media that depend on bad news for their revenue are even starting to become concerned about losing viewers due to the vast amount of negativity that they regurgitate in such phenomenal proportions. While they're not likely to cease this activity—after all, it's the commodity they're selling—they'll probably escalate coverage of what they call the news to another level of shock and chaos. As my friend and direct-mail genius John Hamlin says, "All I need to know about the news I can get from the weather report."

If you are really committed to advancing and conquering, then I suggest that you replace your TV, radio, and newspaper time with programs designed to shift your attention to the positive and solution oriented. For instance, I created a program called Rules of Success that consists of 13 simple steps designed to be executed over the same number of days that will immediately improve your attitude and reset your focus on the exact solution-actions to guarantee your success. In order to truly create your own economy, you must invest every last ounce of energy in the solution, not the problem. This doesn't mean that I don't watch TV at all. I just pick programs that limit the time I spend viewing crisis-type reporting, such as Planet Earth, The Food Network, ball games, or movies of my choice. I feel that this kind of programming allows me to be educated and entertained without feeling down every time I watch TV.

People who abandon positive attitudes might not even be aware of market recovery when it occurs due to the blindness they've adopted and the poor work ethic they've made into a habit. I for one have never met anyone who *didn't* believe in the importance of attitude in terms of its contribution to one's productivity and future. More than 95 percent of all attendees at my seminars and people with whom my company consults believe that they don't do enough to train themselves to be positive and maintain positivity.

However, it's not as simple as instructing someone to "just be positive"—especially in a culture filled with billions of regular negative transmissions. Some books even suggest that simply thinking about what you want will allow you to "attract" those things. While this sounds great, and I believe it is true to some degree, this theory doesn't consider all the other thoughts outside of your awareness that you'll also attract. Telling someone to just be positive in an environment that is very negative is like telling someone who is swimming in the ocean not to get wet. Your friends, coworkers, family members, and others unintentionally but freely contribute negativity to your life each day. You have to counter this type of input with data that will shift your attention to a more solution-oriented outlook. Otherwise, you're apt to pay the price in the form of reduced business. Use my Rules of Success program every morning, and in 13 days, I promise you that your life will be dramatically different. It might be so pronounced that people will ask what you are doing differently! Fill your day with a disciplined schedule and reduce your television intake to recorded programs with no news.

Do something positive every day that makes you feel good. Do it early in the day, during the day, and again in the evening. It could be anything from working out or taking a walk in the morning, to saying something nice to a coworker during the day, to sitting down for a meal and some conversation with your family in the evening. Record your goals at the beginning and end of each day the same way; this will give you two opportunities to pay attention to where you are going. What you give your attention to is what you will end up with. Think poor and you will be poor. Think solutions and you will find many! If you spend more time on advance-and-conquer strategies, you *will* advance and conquer.

Here are some tips for staying positive:

1. Write positive reminders in places you can see in your work environment. Counter negativity with optimistic messages, pictures, and notes.

2. Get on my Rules of Success program for 13 days. This eight-hour program is used over a period of 13 days to shift your thinking and your actions.

3. Exercise each day.

4. Start reading positive books. Try to complete one to three chapters per day.

5. Write down your future goals and dreams daily in present tense as though the goal has been achieved. For example, "I own a helicopter" or "My income is _____."

6. Create and commit to a disciplined schedule, and do not deviate from it.

7. Get an agreement from friends, family, and coworkers to knock off all negativity, and make a game of it. Post a sign at your home or office that says, "*No negativity allowed here!*"

8. Consider getting rid of all toxins, chemicals, and con-
   taminants in your body. All of us store chemicals and
   environmental toxins in our bodies that might be the
   cause of negativity, depression, fear, insecurity, lazi-
   ness, and anxiety. These toxins—accumulated in your
   body's fat cells from poor nutrition and drink choices,
   environmental chemicals, pesticides, prescription
   medicine, drugs, and alcohol—can hinder your mood,
   focus, and energy level. I went through a purification
   process and the results were amazing; I immediately
   had more energy and clearer thoughts.

9. Replace negative thinking with positive thinking.
   Remember that a major problem during all of this
   talk of recession is that *once* people believe there is
   going to be a recession, they start to feel, see, and
   experience those things that are consistent with a
   recession. They then start to exhibit negativity about
   their business prospects and see only what they
   believe. Remember that no matter what you see,
   hear, or read, you ultimately make the choice about
   what you think.

Negative beliefs quickly affect your outlook and the way
you feel about the future prospects of your business. You have
to counter the negativity in the marketplace by replacing it
with positive thinking. Just by asking certain questions, you
can shift your attention from good to bad. Asking *what's wrong
with the economy* often highlights exactly that—what is *wrong*.
But altering that question just a bit by instead asking yourself

what you can do to sell something today immediately shifts your attention to solutions and away from the problem.

One way to get yourself out of a hopeless state is to increase urgency and necessity. For instance, if your life depended on getting a sale today, you would get a sale—regardless of the economy. Take a cue from children; they continue to focus on getting what they want despite any "recession" because they pay more attention to the outcome than the problem. Children will relentlessly pitch as though their lives depend on it—usually until they close the "deal."

Having the most supportive belief structure possible is essential to succeeding in any market and absolutely vital to selling in a tough one. Adopting a winning belief system does not mean that you're in denial. It just means you make the most of every opportunity with a can-do attitude.

There are always opportunities to thrive, regardless of the economic nature of the times. History has countless examples of businesses that found great success during challenging financial circumstances. Ray Kroc bought McDonald's during a recession in 1953 and went on to build the largest fast food restaurant on the planet. Walt Disney went bankrupt several times before developing the largest entertainment company in the world—one that survived the Great Depression and seven recessions. The F. W. Woolworth Company—now known as Foot Locker—was founded with a loan of $300 during the Long Depression, which lasted 23 years. School dropout and child runaway Harland Sanders sold his recipe for Kentucky Fried Chicken after nine years of effort—during two recessions and while living on Social Security checks at the age of 65.

Even in the middle of the darkest economic times, you don't want to have your eyes shut. Be aware, observe, and look for every problem because every problem equals an opportunity. During all times—but especially tough times—people want to work with the most positive and most professional people in the market. Competitors who struggle with negativity translate into more sales for you—if you stay positive.

Be sure you sign up for my "strategy of the week" at www.grantcardone.com. We will send you free strategies with tips on staying positive, expanding, increasing sales, and more. I also offer multiple sales programs on CD and video, even virtual training programs that are available to you 24 hours a day through your computer. These provide training on how to use a positive, solution-oriented sales approach to maximize every opportunity you encounter. These programs have helped thousands of people gain control of their attitudes, make the most of every opportunity, and manage their environments.

Nothing—not your product, service, or company—is more valuable than the ability to maintain and deliver a positive attitude. This influences every area of your life—your physical health, your mental state, and your financial well-being. Money and success are more likely to move toward those who are able to maintain an upbeat, solution-oriented, can-do attitude. Be the placebo effect for yourself and all those around you—and make sure it is a positive effect.

Exercise

An Advance-and-Conquer Attitude

What is the most important thing to avoid during periods of contraction?

_____

_____

_____

What will happen to those who don't keep a good attitude when the market turns around?

_____

_____

_____

What things can you do to stay positive each day?

_____

_____

_____

Write down two examples of people who proved that success is possible even during difficult times and what you admire about them.

1. _____

_____

_____

2. _____

_____

_____

Your Freedom Financial Plan

While some mistakenly say that "the love of money is the root of all evil," I believe it is more accurate to suggest that the lack of *knowledge* about money is the cause of most people's financial problems. So many of us have so much false information regarding money, finance, budgets, debt, and income that it is no wonder that most people never accumulate much wealth. If you misunderstand money, how effective can you possibly be at acquiring or keeping it? Foreclosures, bankruptcies, out-of-control debt, failing businesses, and a government unable to even balance its books all point toward a culture that is either lacking or has incorrect information on the topic of money. I would honestly expect that it is a great deal of both.

I obtained an accounting degree in college because I thought I would be better served in the business world if I understood money, finances, and accounting. But after five years in college, degree in hand, I couldn't get a job, didn't know how to produce income or balance a checkbook, lacked any practical understanding about money or finances—and owed the government $70,000. I think this is the case with most people—whether they have a degree or not. People tend to think that attending college will provide them with this information, but in truth, it often does not.

Most of this country's failing banks are run by individuals who went to some of the highest-ranked, best-known business schools on this planet. Yet they still seem to lack knowledge about how to keep their own businesses viable and solvent. Even people who think they know about money seem a bit confused—and you don't have to look far to see this. People wonder, where do I invest? Do I want debt? Is a home an asset or a liability? What is the difference between a budget and a financial plan? Is *all* credit bad? Should I invest in stocks, bonds, or mutual funds? Is my money safe in the banks? What is an IRA, Keogh, or 401(k)?

I know people who won't buy anything if it isn't on sale yet who are still broke because they don't understand how to produce income. They spend their entire life thinking money is scarce, when in reality, it's merely a currency printed by man. I also know people who know how to produce income but never learn how to manage it and end up with none of it. While most of us believe that money isn't the only element of happiness, we know that it's necessary to maintain a comfortable life. People who go to work every day and earn just enough to pay their bills need not wonder why they aren't motivated. You cannot possibly be driven to succeed if you have no clue what to do with the rewards of your efforts. In order to survive and prosper during a recession, it is vitally important to at least understand the basics about money—including terminology—in order to eliminate confusion. For instance, what is the difference between income and cash flow, "good" and bad debt, or assets and liabilities? The degree to which you understand words is the limit to which you can understand subject matter. (That's why I designed a glossary for the back of this book—so that you can look up new words and increase your understanding of business and financial terminology.)

I know some of the most intelligent people on this planet who ended up dead broke because they were masters at their trade but didn't know how to manage, invest, and make money grow. They were missing an understanding of the very wealth that they worked so hard to amass.

Get a few straightforward books on money, and learn everything you can about the topic. People who have money in the bank and growing investments make better salespeople and businesspeople. They have more confidence and appear more professional because they have their money working for them instead of the other way around. Understanding all the terminology that's used in regard to financial planning, money, finance, savings, and debt won't just make you feel financially secure. It is also the first step to increasing your motivation to reach your goals.

A financial plan differs from a budget and is the basic entry point to creating wealth. It serves as a road map for creating finances and correctly managing your income. It's the financial motivation that takes you to work each day. The first step to take here is to determine your budget, or how much money you currently spend. If you don't already have this in place, then do it now by making a list of everything on which you spent money over the past three months. It will probably help to use your checkbook or credit card statement. Next, figure out how much money you actually *need* to bring in monthly in order to create solvency and get all that you want accomplished. *Solvency* is defined as the ability of an entity to pay its debts with available cash or the ability of a corporation or individual to meet its long-term fixed expenses and accomplish long-term expansion and growth. In other words, the better a company or individual's solvency, the better off it is financially. An insolvent company or individual can no longer operate.

Solvency is a different concept from *profitability*, which refers to the ability to earn a profit. Businesses can be profitable without being solvent (e.g., when they are expanding rapidly); they can even be solvent while losing money (e.g., when they cannibalize future cash flows, like selling accounts receivable). A business is bankrupt when it is unprofitable *and* insolvent.

This is where most people fail with financial planning: They never create a plan that makes them solvent. They spend the lion's share of their time on the budget portion: car payments, mortgage, credit cards, gas/electric bills, other utilities, insurance, food, restaurants, entertainment, dental and medical bills, etc. They completely disregard the more important issues, like future needs, savings, self-improvement, children's educational accounts, vacation funds, home improvement funds, and retirement savings. They're left with only a budget; they never create a financial plan; they spend their lives paying others; and they never get around to funding themselves.

A true financial plan should clearly state your monetary goals. It should outline exactly how you're going to create surpluses of money, what to do with the surpluses, and how to manage and invest that money. A plan suggests that you're doing something to *make things happen*; it's not a historic evaluation of what has been done already (a budget). *Plan* means a method of achieving an end, a strategy of how one is going to stay viable and solvent as a household or a business. A budget is a list of all those things on which you're spending money. Clipping coupons, saving money, cutting back, and anything to do with controlling expenses is all about a budget whereas a financial plan focuses on wealth *creation*.

One of the reasons why people never seem to have enough money is that they focus their attention on a budget instead of a plan. You need to ask yourself the following questions: How much money do we really need in order to live? How much do we need in order to fund future retirement plans, vacations, education for children, savings, investments, etc.? Who has the money to fund those activities? How much activity will be needed to create that kind of money? A financial plan is the expansion consideration, not the contraction (budget) consideration. It lays out how you are going to reach your goals, make your dreams come true, and have the future you desire; it's the motivation for going to work in the first place.

During tough times, your customers will have their attention pinned down in the same area as everyone else and will of course be more reluctant to make purchases. Since they're also focusing on their budget, you have to do a better job at "unpinning" them by showing how your products and services can help them expand. The degree to which you have a complete understanding of how much money you actually need in order to create the future you want will determine how successful you are in selling over these objections. The more dedicated you are to designing a financial plan, the more clearly you can focus on how much money you must create in order to pay yourself (not just the creditors)—something that will inevitably lead to your success in the marketplace.

So take some time to determine how much money you actually need and all the potential sources available to you: your power base, past clients, people to whom you have been unsuccessful in selling—basically anyone who can contribute to your financial plan. Don't forget that even during periods of economic contraction, there are still people who have money and will spend it. After all, there is no shortage of money on Earth; there is a shortage of planning, motivation, courage, action, and follow-through. Your own personal lack of wealth merely means that you don't understand something or don't have the correct motivation. Once you put a financial plan in place, you will spend the rest of your energy finding those people who need your products and services—people who will fund your financial plan and help you advance and conquer.

Exercise

Your Freedom Financial Plan

What is the major difference between a financial plan and a budget?

_____
_____
_____

To what does a financial plan provide basic entry?

_____
_____
_____

Why does a person who has a financial plan make a better salesperson than one who does not?

_____
_____
_____

Give four examples of why you can tell that there is *not* a shortage of money on the planet.

1. _____
_____
_____

2. _____
_____
_____

(continued)

(*continued*)

3. _____

_____

_____

4. _____

_____

_____

The Most Important Skill Needed to Advance and Conquer

Your sales, communication, negotiating, and closing skills are vital to your achievement in order for you to advance and conquer. You can't take market share unless you can sell your ideas, products, and services. Every profession has a skill set. A carpenter needs a hammer, nails, and lumber, and—to the degree he knows his trade—he will be desirable in the marketplace. A farmer needs a tractor, seed, trucks, fertilizer, water, fuel, etc. A boxer needs a good jab, a great hook, solid defense, stamina to go 12 rounds, footwork, and a fight plan. A chef needs proper utensils, recipes, seasoning, food, refrigerators, stoves, ovens, and warmers.

When things are tough, you and your company need—more than anything else—organizational, management, and planning skills and the ability to sell your products and services. You could fail as a manager, but if you were able to sell enough of your products and smartly control your money, you could still be successful. You can plan and organize until you're blue in the face, but if you can't sell your products, what does it matter how organized you are?

Most of us don't have a line of people waiting for our products; we actually have to generate interest, sell our product, and close the deal. The lifeblood of every company is revenue, and revenue is generated by sales. Therefore, every organization's most necessary assets—that

alone can determine its success (or lack thereof)—are the
sales skills of its employees.

Developing sales skills involves communication, motivation, belief in your product, a great attitude, presentation
skills, the ability to negotiate and close the deal, follow-up,
and the creation of new and qualified opportunities. Selling is to an organization what food, water, and oxygen are
to the body. Businesspeople sometimes exhibit a disdain at
the notion of being labeled a salesperson, but this is a critical error. This disdain is a result of never taking the time
to learn the mechanics and true art of selling. Many people
were able to avoid selling due to demand for their product
or because of a period of time of careless spending and free
credit. But there comes a time in every person's career where
you will either learn the skill of selling or give up any hope of
ever being first. Even those who consider themselves to
be professional salespeople usually only learn a few basics
about their craft and never perfect all the tools available to
them. I am not talking about selling as an activity here, but
the ultimate way to dominate and ensure yourself the top
seat in the marketplace.

Most salespeople typically learn a few fundamental
skills in the first 90 days or so—and then spend the rest
of their careers operating under this initial, foundational
knowledge. If a boxer took that approach, he would never
make it to a paid fight, regardless of his natural abilities.
Despite the myth, *no one* is "born a salesman." I am an
expert in sales, but trust me I was not born a salesperson.
I was born a baby like everyone else and have the photos

to prove it. No one I have ever met has been instilled with closing skills—these are developed. While some people have a natural ability to build a rapport that lends itself to the profession of selling, they won't become masters at the art of bringing in revenue unless they develop a full set of skills. A lot of salespeople become good enough to call themselves professionals but avoid spending the time to become experts—and that is a big mistake. Even professionals can spend a career destroying opportunities and then go home and complain about how tough selling is. And that is during good times! When the economy gets tough, the complaining gets louder, the pain becomes intensified, and many salespeople become statistics—and only after it is too late, they wish they would have prepared more.

A daunting economic situation usually means too much time and not enough sales. Those who really understand selling as a science and a technology—and who spend time to develop and perfect their entire set of sales skills—are the people who will realize success. Salespeople of this caliber stand to benefit from contracting markets; there will be more business for them as their competition falls by the wayside. Consistent sales results will not go to the mediocre, the average, the weak, or the order takers. Business ends up in the hands of the professional or those willing to give their products and services away, and the latter clearly won't be around for long. Mediocre salespeople *always* face challenges during periods of contraction.

So wake up and realize that you cannot survive and prosper if you don't learn to sell yourself, your products, services, ideas, and dreams. This holds true for everyone, regardless of his or her position. Selling is not a *job*; it's something you do in order to make things happen for yourself.

Now is the time to hammer down and work daily on training, education, and improving your sales skills. I suggest that you do this no matter what position you have in your organization. People who can generate or assist in the generation of sales and revenue will never be without work, money, or opportunity. You must commit to understanding selling as a technology, a system, and an art and commit to becoming an expert as a way to the top not approach it merely as a job.

Take every opportunity and free moment you have to learn the art of selling. Use the time you spend commuting to and from work each day to listen to material on generating revenue for yourself and your company. Call my office and let us show you how to turn your car or computer into a schoolhouse on learning to close deals. We can hook into your computer and stream virtual sales motivation, solutions, coaching, and training to you 24/7. Call my office for a free demonstration of our virtual sales training. I assure you it will blow your mind. Start focusing your attention on growing your business, using objections as a way to close more deals, negotiating strategies that will double your gross selling volumes, and how to leave your competitors in the dust. Every action that precedes this chapter is dependent upon your understanding and confidence in your ability to sell. There is no skill set more vital to ensuring that you advance and conquer.

Visit www.virtualsalestraining.com to find out more.

Remember that after long periods of prosperity, businesses get used to taking orders and tend to forget about selling. Any weaknesses in this most necessary skill—and even the company's sales processes—are easy to overlook during periods of economic expansion. Some level of success is always achieved due to the ease with which people spend and invest. During periods of contraction, however, every shortcoming is magnified and results in lost opportunities and vital revenue. Starting in the mid-1980s, companies, entire industries, and sales ventures began to depend on mass marketing in order to drive traffic and produce sales. But extensive advertising budgets aren't cost effective during contractions, so it's back to a period of a smaller number of opportunities. And you had better make the most of each one because you need the revenue. This is when it's absolutely critical to learn (maybe relearn) everything there is to know about creating selling opportunities, determining your prospects' motives, getting agreement, presenting, negotiating, and closing. Periods of slowdown are the time to train, not the time to complain.

For 25 years, I have made myself a student of selling. I've tried to learn everything I can about selling as a technology and an art, not just a position. Because of that commitment, I ended up with a career instead of a job—and there is a great deal of difference between the two. Through my personal research, I have determined that there has been very little written on selling over the past 50 years that is different or unique. I therefore came up with Information-Assisted Selling™. There are new advances in sales today that I have validated in the marketplace and proved to be more effective than many of yesterday's worn-out strategies. These improvements have been used to revolutionize entire industries, revitalize thousands of businesses, and energize hundreds of thousands of individuals. There is not an industry on this planet that does not change in some way or another, and those that don't change simply cease to exist. I broke the selling code in the twenty-first century by creating new ways to handle people in order to get your products sold—no matter what is going on with the economy. These breakthroughs have not just augmented sales results; they've increased customer satisfaction, shortened sales cycles, and improved employee retention. I have been personally contacted by thousands of people who once thought that after spending a career in selling, going to seminars, and reading books, they knew it all—but have been blown away by these new developments. My books, audio and video programs, sales training virtual technology, online programs, schools, and seminars will make you a master at the art of selling—despite the economy, competition, or what personality type you have.

Vincent Van Gogh—one of the greatest artists who ever lived—sold only a single painting of the hundreds he painted during his lifetime. This was an individual who produced some of the greatest art in the last 2,000 years, but because of his inability or unwillingness to sell, his brilliance didn't generate any revenue until long after his death. This goes to show you that no matter how exceptional your product, you won't benefit financially if you can't sell it.

Because of the increased competition that has accompanied the Information Age, the twenty-first-century buyer is much more knowledgeable, educated, selective, and certainly resistant to old-school approaches. Combine all of that with a contracting economy and lowest-price competitors who are "selling scared," and your job of advancing your products and ideas in the marketplace becomes even more challenging.

As I mentioned previously, I began my first sales job in 1983 during a period of massive economic contraction. I was working in a highly competitive industry selling products that were not, for the most part, "must-have" items. Most of the individuals and companies either couldn't afford my product or had reasons to delay purchasing it. But because I trained daily—even fanatically—to improve my skills, I would sometimes outsell the entire sales staff. In just one year, I had actually reached the top 1 percent in the entire industry in which I worked. Why? Not because I was a born salesperson but because I prepared daily on how to make the most of every opportunity in which I was engaged. Sales training, or what we like to call *sales effectiveness*, does not cost money; it connects you with the money you need during tough times in order to advance and conquer. You cannot afford to miss opportunities now; you have to be in perfect shape to take advantage of every day and every opportunity and be able to close every sale.

A lot of people worry about how to spend their money. However, they would be better served if they focused on improving their skills in order to earn *more* money and take advantage of every opportunity. The most successful people I've encountered concentrate on making the most of every opportunity they have to produce money. Advance and conquer; don't retreat and save. You will waste more money in your lifetime on missed opportunities than you will ever spend. Investing in your education, learning how to communicate, and negotiating and closing transactions are the only ways to move forward.

Remember the rule of *no*. Whenever you say *no* to something in life, there is usually a lack of *know*. If you have no money, there is something you don't *know* about money. If you have no prospects, there is something you don't *know* about prospecting. If you find yourself with no closes, there is something you don't know about closing.

The degree to which you know how to sell encompasses your ability to effectively communicate, attain an agreement, handle objections, be likeable, generate opportunities, give great product demonstrations, negotiate, and know how to close. It is naïve to think that you can train someone who doesn't know how to sell, communicate, negotiate, and close deals. Why would a person pursue prospects when he or she doesn't know what to do with them?

If you have not read my book *Sell to Survive* (www.selltosurvive.com), get it immediately. It will rehabilitate your skills as a salesperson and emphasizes the importance of selling to your future and your survival regardless of the economy or your title. No dream, idea, product, or service—no matter how good it is—will make it to the marketplace without someone to sell it. Your future, financial well-being and even job security are determined by your ability to create opportunities for your company and drive revenue through selling. Anyone who cannot generate opportunities or directly bring revenue to the company during periods of downturn will be the first to lose his or her job. The most needed and protected people in the workforce are those who can sell and bring in the money.

Despite what you may have been told, *everyone* sells at one time or another. Even A-list movie stars who are at the very top of their careers have to assist in selling their movies; if no one buys tickets, the studios will quit making movies with them. The president of the United States sells his or her way to the White House and, once there, must continue to sell in order to get his programs in place and get reelected.

Business schools state that the number one reason why companies and individuals fail is because they are undercapitalized; in other words, they don't have cash. I don't believe this to be true. People and organizations fail because they aren't able to effectively sell their products and services in quantities great enough—and at prices high enough—to remain viable.

So whatever your job title or position may be, I plead with you to learn everything you can about this great lost art. It is the only way you'll advance and conquer and never be stopped by something as trivial as the condition of the economy.

Exercise

The Most Important Skill Needed to Advance and Conquer

What is your most important skill and why?

_____
_____
_____

What are the seven skills of a salesperson?

1. _____
   _____
   _____

2. _____
   _____
   _____

3. _____
   _____
   _____

4. _____
   _____
   _____

5. _____
   _____
   _____

6. _____

_____

_____

7. _____

_____

_____

What is the only thing that costs money?

_____

_____

_____

What is the only reason why individuals and businesses fail? (full quote)

_____

_____

_____

Become a master at selling.

Visit www.grantcardone.com/resources

19

The Unreasonable Attitude

I have spent the past 18 chapters explaining the tactics that are necessary to advance and conquer in a struggling economy. What I want to do now is convince you to execute these actions as though your life completely depended upon each of them. I want you to shift into a level of operation whereby you throw away much of your social upbringing and training and develop the tendency and even preference to be completely unreasonable with these actions. Those who will succeed in the marketplace, especially during economic contractions, are the rule breakers, the noisemakers, the attention getters—the unreasonable ones. They are the "untouchables" who regularly do things that set them apart from the economy as a whole. Those who remain sensible become victims of economic swings and competition while those who act irrationally will expand, conquer, and grab market share.

Contrary to what Frank Sinatra claims in his song "My Way," most people will have many regrets in their lifetime—not just a few. I expect that a fair number of individuals will look back and wish they had done more—not less—and really gone after their dreams with more energy, tenacity, and an unreasonable level of effort. I also think most will wish in hindsight that they had "swung for the fences," taken the big gamble, and really put themselves all out there. So why wait until the end of your life to wish for these things?

Start now, and approach every day as though your future depends upon an almost insane-like pursuit of success.

When I say *insane* here, I simply mean over the top, operating without the usual logic or reason that has a tendency to constrain people. I don't want to respond as others would; I just want to get the job done. Behaving in this way means going forth without editing or judging your behavior based on how everyone else acts but instead on what it takes to accomplish the task at hand.

Social means "marked by or passed in pleasant companionship with one's friends or associates." A *norm* is defined as "a principle of right action binding upon the members of a group and serving to guide, control, or regulate proper and acceptable behavior." Put together, you have social norm—one of the major reasons why people elect *not* to take the actions necessary to create the life they want. It's a shame to see so many people doing solely what is necessary in order to survive when they have their backs against the wall. I have met thousands of extremely successful people, none of whom ever claimed that their success came easily to them. They all share the common purpose of making their dreams and goals a reality, and many of them did not truly experience their brilliance until they realized that the fulfillment of their dreams required them to act unreasonably. That purpose seems to fuel their willingness to be irrational, even to go against social norms at times. Consider this: Had the Founding Fathers of the United States conformed to the social norms of England, they would have ended up in prison instead of building a new country.

Unreasonable people are often criticized for being so eager to challenge societal barriers. But those who stand by their actions and get things accomplished—despite the negativity, ridicule, and fear they endure—will eventually lose their label as an outcast and instead receive admiration. These people are content to make their own rules; they risk breaking the rules in order to build the life, business, industry, and economy they want. Anyone who has contributed at exceptional levels has at some point in his or her life acted irrationally—and been ridiculed, even condemned for it.

For example, where would Christianity be without the teachings, stories, and examples left to us by the life of Jesus Christ? He was willing to be ridiculed and even had to leave his own land in order to get others to listen to him. What if the Founding Fathers had not fought against the powers of England? What if Dr. Martin Luther King Jr. had decided to abide by the laws of his day and never made himself heard? More recently—and on a somewhat smaller scale—what if Howard Schultz had taken the advice of his father-in-law and abandoned his dream to build Starbucks? People weren't requesting coffee shops on every corner, after all. What if Bill Gates had listened to his father and remained at Harvard? He might not have founded Microsoft and become one of the richest men in the world. What if Mother Teresa had not spent her whole life dedicated to her causes? She would not have saved the countless lives nor made the impact on this planet that she did. Where would the world be if the Wright Brothers had not insanely and unreasonably continued their pursuit of flight?

What if Barack Obama had listened to what many said was "impossible"? He would not have become the first African American president of the United States.

I could go on and on, listing examples of people who refused to quit and follow societal conventions in order to realize their dreams. *The economy you have is only limited by the amount of unreasonable action you take to create it.* During periods of economic contraction, you must refuse to agree with any social norms that hold you back. Of course, you want to avoid anything that will get you into trouble or hurt other people. But barring those scenarios, think about some of the rules you blindly follow—and what might be different if you didn't. Those who are able to utilize the childlike ability to disagree, go against the tide, and act illogically will be ensured success, despite economic conditions. I encourage you to (1) disagree with the masses; and (2) go overboard with your actions. It certainly won't be easy. You'll have to throw off what you consider appropriate and acceptable. You'll probably receive some criticism, judgment, and even ridicule. These reactions are simply indications that you're on the right track.

Most people spend their lives receiving too little attention, with no one ever noticing them. Creating the life you want requires that you demand others' attention. You want people to be talking about you because otherwise, no one will ever know about you, your products, or your services. And the only trouble you will get from being unreasonable is envy on the part of others—as well as financial freedom. If you don't stand out, you probably will not be left standing during serious economic contractions.

Show me someone who did something exceptional, and I will show you an exceptional person—a case to which a rule does not apply. To do something out of the ordinary, you have to act that way. Now is the time to get attention, go the extra mile, break free from the masses, do what others refuse to do, and be unreasonable in your thinking and actions.

Exercise

The Unreasonable Attitude

What are the four types of people who will succeed in the marketplace?

1. _____
   _____
   _____

2. _____
   _____
   _____

3. _____
   _____
   _____

4. _____
   _____
   _____

(continued)

(*continued*)

What are the four things that you should not concern yourself with at this time?

1. _____
   _____
   _____

2. _____
   _____
   _____

3. _____
   _____
   _____

4. _____
   _____
   _____

List three examples of people who operated irrationally in order to create something.

1. _____
   _____
   _____

2. _____
   _____
   _____

3. _____
   _____
   _____

Write down two things you would regret if your life ended today.

1. _____

_____

_____

2. _____

_____

_____

What are three ways in which you could start operating in a more "insane-like" manner?

1. _____

_____

_____

2. _____

_____

_____

3. _____

_____

_____

Learn how to have an "unreasonable" attitude.
Visit www.grantcardone.com/resources

How to Guarantee Your Position

feel that it's now my job to inspire you to actually implement and execute these actions. Let's face it: The big, bad, vast economy is not going to accommodate you with more opportunities and more business without you taking some serious initial steps. The economy most likely doesn't even know you exist; up until now, you only operated as a small part of the economy and probably never gave a thought to creating your own. The government is not going to bail you out, and it certainly is not going to help you and your company advance and conquer. (In fact, if it offered to, you would probably be better off resisting.) The "money gods" aren't going to guarantee your solvency or financial freedom, no matter how hard you pray to them. The economy is in the state it's in; you can be part of it and get whatever is left over after billions of people take their piece, or you can create your own and no longer be a victim of it.

Taking the time to pick up this book and read it suggests that you truly do want to do something different. For this, I acknowledge and congratulate you. Well done to you on getting the book. I applaud you for reading it and even more for finishing it. Now, if you want the world to give you a standing ovation, put the lessons in it to work.

Interestingly, one of the most effective ways of perfecting these disciplines is to help others attain success and implement these actions themselves. When people with common goals and motivations come together, they tend to learn faster and become a support system for one another. So gather a group of like-minded, "unreasonable," and highly driven people who refuse to live by the social norms of the mediocre. Spend time with others who demand to be *first* in the market and who desire to advance and conquer as much as you do. Assemble a study group to read this book and do the exercises with you. If you own a company, ask your employees to read this book as a team. Then help one another apply and commit to using the actions—and hold one another accountable to these commitments. Go through one chapter per week in a study and discussion session, and follow the recorded audio program. Take the time to look up words in the glossary and really evaluate what each of them means. Teaching others and being part of a group will galvanize your understanding of the material. It will increase your need to perfect what you've learned and prove it workable in the marketplace. It will also immediately connect you with other like-minded people who want to improve their futures, and it will extend your power base.

Something tells me that you didn't pick up this book because you are comfortable or satisfied with where you are in life. Chances are you want to change or improve your current position; this will require that you engage in actions that are outside your comfort zone. You won't find it easy to execute these techniques at first because you're doing something new. If you aren't at least a little bit uncomfortable, then you're likely only doing more of what you have done before, not taking new actions that will incite growth.

There are disciplines you must pursue in order to be *first*, and these require a new mind-set about how to build your business and create your own economy. The discomforts you experience now may well guarantee that you'll be comfortable in the future.

So I hope you elect to be uncomfortable—at least for awhile. Go out there and break through the social norms that your education, family, and the media taught you. Stay with each of the actions until each becomes such a habit that you no longer even see it as being exceptional. Any action alone will get you great results; all of them together will get you phenomenal ones.

I even hope that you're ridiculed, judged, and mocked a bit because if you are willing to go to those lengths, you will reach every financial and personal goal you've set. Tough economies are not "normal" times, so stop worrying about being normal. When the economic slowdown ends—and I promise, at some point, it will—you will have developed a skill set that no one else has, a mind-set above those with whom you compete, a superior advantage in the marketplace, and hopefully, an economy of your own that doesn't depend on outside sources. This will not be a sprint but a marathon of forming new habits and honing a discipline that will become a way of life for you.

I suggest that you become a fanatic of each of these actions and use them in a completely unreasonable way. Don't worry about logic; take action as though your life depends on it—because it does. Your financial life, personal confidence, and overall outlook all depend on the results you attain in the marketplace. The economy does not control people; we compose and control it. Your financial situation is the sum total of the actions you take each day. I have great hopes for you, and I encourage you to take the information herein and use it to ensure that your actions—not the marketplace—determine your, your family, and your company's financial future.

Be outrageous in your thinking, relentless in your execution, and unreasonable in your actions, and you too will advance and conquer.

Afterword

Regardless of whether you are just starting out, have been in business for awhile, or are a veteran of the business world, my hope is that this book inspires you to make some changes. Change requires actions, not just ideas. Make the material in this book part of your daily operations, and it will take you to another level of success.

Whether you are riding the wave of some great opportunity or in the midst of an economic contraction, the technologies and actions found here will either advance the wave you are on or allow you to advance and conquer while others become victims. Whatever the negative conditions in which you find yourself, the right actions—performed consistently—will help you along your way.

I don't want you to be one of those people just "getting by," constantly afraid and uncertain about the market. I want you to be above the scene and independent of what is going on around you. This book should be used as a reference guide for you and your organization to measure what you are doing weekly and monthly to make you bigger, better, faster, and stronger. Whether your goal is merely to secure you and your family's future or to dominate and take market share from your competitors, this book will show you how to do it.

Be careful not to underestimate these tools because they seem obvious or simple. The most effective tools usually are. And don't just read this book one time; you will change with your experiences, and you will see new ways to use this material each time you read it.

While the rest of the world is preoccupied with problems, your job now is to fill your every thought and action with the solutions that will allow you to advance. I am greatly interested in the success you find from using this information, and I welcome your calls and e-mails. I also want to know what difficulties you encounter. If you have questions or challenges while executing any of these actions or run into situations that you do not know how to handle, please contact my office at 1-800-368-5771 or e-mail me at gc@grantcardone.com.

Prepare yourself for a great adventure, advancing to new heights and conquering new territories and dreams! May the actions you take daily set a good example for those around you. Let others see that anything is possible when you have focus and the correct information—and when you take the right actions!

Be Deaf when Someone Says You Can't!

Grant Cardone

Be deaf when someone says you cannot do it!
Be deaf when someone says it is impossible!
Be deaf when anyone tries to put limits on you!
For these people who make efforts to limit you and suggest that
you cannot fulfill your dreams are dangerous people.
These people have given up on their dreams
and seek to convince you to do the same.
And do not be confused by them when they suggest
that they are only trying to help you!
Help is not what they offer.
What they really seek to do is have you join the ranks of slaves,
the apathetic, and the hopeless.
Be deaf to all of them!

Glossary

This is not a complete glossary by any means, and I have only given you the definition in which the word was used in this book. Most words have multiple meanings, so for a full understanding of each word, seek out a good dictionary. Your ability to fully understand any subject is limited only by your understanding of the words contained in that subject. Further, your action is limited by your understanding.

401(k). A retirement account to which both employee and employer contribute, taxes are deferred until withdrawal.

absolute. Positive, unquestionable, or in total.

abundance. (1) So much you can never be without, quantity; (2) affluence, wealth.

accommodate. (1) To bring into agreement or concord; (2) help out or serve.

accomplish. (1) Succeed, bring about by effort; (2) bring to completion; (3) to succeed or overcome something.

act. (1) The doing of a something, short for action; (2) something done with the intent of accomplishing something.

action. (1) Things done in order to get results; (2) things usually done over a period of time, in stages, or with the possibility of repetition.

adapt. Change, or to make fit (as for a specific or new use or situation), often by modification.

additional. Adding, something more, an increase.

advertising. The action of bringing something to the attention of the public. This can be done by word of mouth, signage, TV, radio, print, direct mail, publications, newsletter, YouTube, video, social media, and so on.

agreed. (1) To move into the same direction of others' beliefs; (2) concede.

agreement. (1) Verbal or written contract executed and legally binding; (2) the language or instrument laying out those things agreed upon.

air. (1) The general character or sense of anything; (2) overall consensus or feeling of those in attendance.

a la carte. Each item is priced separately and decided on as separate items. Typically used in selling to build value.

alterations. The result of changing or modifying to make different without changing into something else.

Amway. A direct-selling company that uses independent contractors to market, also known as multilevel marketing or network marketing to promote its products. Amway was founded in 1959 by Jay Van Andel and Richard DeVos. Based in Ada, Michigan, the company and family of companies reported sales growth of 15 percent, reaching $8.4 billion for the year ending

December 31, 2008, marking the company's seventh straight year of growth. Its product lines include thousands of home care products.

ancillary. Supplementary.

annual. A period of a year.

apathetic. (1) Attitude of quitting or giving up; (2) having or showing little or no feeling or emotion; spiritless.

apathy. Lack of interest or concern; below bored.

arrogance. An attitude of better than, often manifested by presumptuous claims or assumptions.

assertive. Characterized by boldness or confidence, takes charge, and confident of the direction that needs to be taken.

asset. An item of value owned; or some personal quality that is a benefit to you. (i.e., His smile was an asset greater than his financial assets.)

assignments. Task given to either accomplish something or learn something.

attention. (1) What you focus on the most; (2) consideration of the needs and wants of others.

audition. A trial performance to qualify an entertainer's ability to be right for a role.

bank collapse. Failing of a bank that causes it to close.

bank run. Occurs when a large number of bank customers withdraw their deposits at the same time because they believe the bank is, or might become, insolvent.

bankruptcy. (1) A legal action a person or company will take in order to resolve its inability to pay its creditors; (2) a person or company who becomes insolvent.

barrage. Vigorous or rapid outpouring or projection of many things or actions at one time.

basic. The starting point.

basics. Something that is fundamental (get back to *basics*).

Basil King. William Benjamin Basil King (1859–1928) was a Canadian-born clergyman who became a writer after retiring from the clergy.

bend over backward. Go beyond the normal expectations in order to create a positive effect or provide extra service or make an impression.

beyond. (1) To the farther side, more, extra; (2) in addition to what is expected.

Bible. Books of the central religious text of Judaism and Christianity.

biochemical. Something to do with chemical reactions in living organisms.

biological. Study of living organisms and vital processes.

BlackBerry. A wireless handheld device introduced in 1999 as a two-way pager. In 2002, known more commonly as the smart phone. BlackBerry supports push e-mail, mobile telephone, text messaging, Internet faxing, Web browsing, and other wireless information services, as well as a multitouch interface.

blind. (1) Without sight of certain objects or knowledge of certain facts that could serve for guidance or cause bias; (2) having no knowledge of information. (i.e., like a blind test).

blip. Something relatively small or inconsequential.

block and tackle. A term used to simply state doing those simple necessary things in order to accomplish a task (comes from football terminology).

bogeyman. (1) Something that does not exist that scares people; (2) a legendary ghost-like monster.

briefing. Giving short precise instructions or essential information.

broke. (1) To ruin financially; (2) run out of something usually money.

budget. Generally is a list of all expenses and incoming money. The purpose of a budget is to plan for saving and spending.

business downturn. A downward turn in the statistics, especially a decline in business and economic activity.

buy-in. Signifies the commitment of affected parties to "buy in" to the decision; that is, to agree to give it support.

campaign. A connected series of actions meant to bring about a particular result.

capital. (1) Accumulated goods, in contrast to income; *also* the value of these accumulated goods; (2) accumulated goods devoted to the production of other valuable goods or that bring in income

chaos. A state of complete confusion.

cheerleader. A person who directs cheering and goodwill for a team, person, and so on, as they work toward a goal.

church activities. A form of organized, extracurricular recreation in a place of worship.

Circuit City. Publicly held company that sold electronics. Failed in 2009.

circumstance. Essential and environmental factors in a situation.

cold call. A call made without introduction or advance notice, referred to as "cold" because no introduction has been made.

community. A body of persons of common interests.

competitive. Striving consciously or unconsciously toward a goal.

conditioned. Brought or put into a specified state by a number of exact steps.

conquer. To gain mastery over something by overcoming obstacles.

contact. *(noun)* A person serving as a go-between, messenger, connection, or source of special information (business *contacts*).

contact. *(verb)* To get in communication with.

contraction. (1) The act of getting smaller; (2) reducing efforts and resources.

control. To exercise restraining or directing influence over someone or something.

counterintuitive. Contrary to what one would intuitively expect.

courage. An act that demonstrates the mental or moral strength to persevere and withstand danger, fear, or difficulty.

craft. An occupation or trade requiring manual dexterity or artistic skill.

crawfish. A small, freshwater crustacean resembling the lobster. This is a famous food of Louisiana that is boiled and when you visit there, be sure you try it. They are delicious but very messy.

creative. Having the quality of something created rather than imitated.

critical. Of, relating to, or being a turning point or an especially important juncture.

crossover. An instance of breaking into another category.

cultivate. To encourage and promote growth.

culture. The set of shared attitudes, values, and practices of a group, ethnicity, organization, or institution.

CRM (customer relationship management). Software applications that allow companies to manage every aspect of their relationship with a customer. The aim of these systems is to assist in building lasting customer relationships—to turn customer satisfaction into customer loyalty. Customer information acquired from sales, marketing, customer service, and support is captured and stored in a centralized database. The system may provide data-mining facilities that support an opportunity management system. It may also be integrated with other systems such as accounting and manufacturing for a truly enterprise-wide system with thousands of users.

customer satisfaction. (business term) A measure of how products and services supplied by a company meet or surpass customer expectations. It is seen as a key performance indicator within business and is part of the four perspectives of a balanced scorecard.

cycle (sales cycle). An interval of time when a sequence of events is completed.

database. A usually large collection of data organized especially for rapid search and retrieval.

database management. The act of conducting or supervising of usually a large collection of data.

data-scrubbing programs. The process of taking a data set with individually identifiable information and removing or altering the data in such a way that the usefulness of the data set is retained, but the identification of individuals contained in that data set is nearly impossible.

dazzling. To arouse admiration by an impressive display.

deaf ears. Unwilling to hear or listen; not to be persuaded.

deal. An arrangement for mutual advantage.

defy. To confront with strong resistance; to disregard.

degree. The relative intensity of something.

delusion. Act of misleading the mind or judgment of something. (I used this in the context of misleading yourself from falsehoods—in this way, delusion is good.)

demise. A cessation of existence or of some activity.

demographics. The statistical characteristics of human populations as age or income used especially to identify markets.

denial. A psychological defense mechanism in which confrontation with a personal problem or with reality is avoided by denying the existence of the problem or reality.

dependency. The quality or state of relying on something, or of having an addiction.

deploy. To spread out, utilize, or arrange for a deliberate purpose.

deprived. Not having enough of the necessities of life.

determine. To decide conclusively (*determine* motives).

detox. To remove a harmful poison or toxin from the body.

diminish. To make less or cause to appear less.

discipline. To train or develop by instruction and exercise, especially in self-control.

differentiate. To mark or show a difference in, constitute a difference that distinguishes.

diligence. Characterized by steady, earnest, and energetic efforts.

Dillard's. A major chain of department stores in the United States.

direct mail. Printed matter (as circulars) prepared for soliciting business or contributions and mailed directly to individuals. Typically, this refers to programs where entire databases are mailed to with a particular offer.

disagreeable. Can describe a person who is able to disagree with the acceptable norm or social considerations.

dissertation. An extended, usually written, writing on a subject.

do nots. A made-up word—things you want to avoid or not do.

dollar store. A variety store that sells inexpensive items, usually with a single price point for all items in the store. Typical merchandise includes cleaning supplies, toys, and confectionary.

double down. Term from the game blackjack whereby you double your previous bet in hopes of either doubling your winnings or making up your losses.

downside. A negative aspect, worst-case scenario.

downturn. A downward turn, especially toward a decline in business and economic activity.

earn. (1) To become worthy of or entitled or suited to; (2) to make worthy of or obtain (*earn* your business).

economic contraction. A shrinking or lessening relating to, or based on, the production, distribution, and consumption of goods and services.

economy. The structure or conditions relating to, or based on the production, distribution, and consumption of goods and services in a country, area, or period. A country, company, and even an individual has an economy.

effective. Producing a decided, decisive, or desired effect.

elated. Marked by high spirits, exultant.

encourage. To give help or patronage to (*encourage* others to do business with you).

end-all. Describes the ultimate solution.

endurance. The ability to withstand hardship or adversity; *especially* the ability to sustain a prolonged stressful effort or activity.

enlist. To secure the support and aid of; employ in advancing an interest.

entrée. The main course of a meal in the United States.

environment. The circumstances, objects, or conditions by which one is surrounded.

erode. To cause to deteriorate or disappear as if by eating or wearing away.

exception. A case to which a rule does not apply.

exhibit. To present to view, as to show or display outwardly, especially by visible signs or actions.

expand. To increase the extent, number, volume, or scope of, enlarge (comes from *spread*).

expansion. Act of increasing the extent, number, volume, or scope of something.

experience. (1) Direct observation of or participation in events as a basis of knowledge; (2) the fact of having gained knowledge through direct observation or participation.

exploit. To utilize something. (Often the connotation is to make use of something or someone in a mean or unfair way.)

extra mile. More than is usual or necessary.

fanatic. (1) Marked by excessive enthusiasm and often intense; (2) uncritical devotion.

financial plan. A plan of how to stay solvent in regard to income and expenses.

first quarter. The first three months of a financial year.

flier. An advertising circular.

***Fortune* 500.** Top 500 companies in the United States based on gross sales.

freelancer. A person who acts independently without being affiliated with an organization or employer.

fuel. In this usage, I mean to "stimulate" something (*fuel* the fires of action).

funk. To be in a collapse, or a slump.

F. W. Woolworth. A retail company that was one of the original American five-and-dime stores (often referred to as Woolworth's). It grew to be one of the largest retail chains in the world through most of the twentieth century, but increased competition led to its decline beginning in the 1980s.

Gates, Bill. American business magnate, philanthropist, author, and chairman of Microsoft, the software company he founded with Paul Allen. He is ranked consistently one of the world's wealthiest people and the wealthiest overall as of March 2009. During his career at Microsoft, Gates held the positions of CEO and chief software architect, and he remains the largest individual shareholder with more than 8 percent of the common stock.

generate. To create or be the cause of a situation, action, or state of mind.

genuine. Free from hypocrisy or pretense, sincere.

goals. The end toward which effort is directed.

Google. A corporation that earns revenue from advertising related to its Internet search, e-mail, online mapping, office productivity, social networking, and video-sharing services.

Great Depression. A worldwide economic downturn starting in most places in 1929 and ending at different times in the 1930s or early 1940s for different countries. It was the largest and most important economic depression in the twentieth century and is used in the twenty-first century as an example of how far the world's economy can fall. The Great Depression originated in the United States; historians most often use as a starting date the stock market crash on October 29, 1929, known as Black Tuesday.

GDP (gross domestic product). One of the measures of national income and output for a given country's economy. It is the total value of all final goods and services produced in a particular economy—the dollar value of all goods and services produced within a country's borders in a given year. GDP can be defined in three ways, all of which are conceptually identical. First, it is equal to the total expenditures for all final goods and services produced within the country in a stipulated period of time (usually a 365-day year). Second, it is equal to the sum of the value added at every stage of production (the intermediate stages) by all the industries within a country, plus taxes, less subsidies on products, in the period. Third, it is equal to the sum of the income generated by production in the country in the period—that is, compensation of employees, taxes on production, and imports less subsidies and gross operating surplus (or profits).

guarantee. An assurance for the fulfillment of a condition.

gullible. Easily duped or cheated.

hammer. To strike or drive with a force suggesting the blow of a hammer.

Heard Automotive. Founded by Bill Heard, who operated the largest Chevrolet franchise in the world—he closed all operations in 2009.

HerbaLife. Founded in 1980, a company that sells weight-loss, nutrition, and skin-care products by multilevel marketing, also known as network marketing. It has been the subject of controversy and lawsuits.

high-handed. Showing no regard for the rights or feelings of others.

high margin. A product (or service) that has larger profits.

hot stuff. Description of something or someone that is on their game.

huddle. To gather in a close pack for the sake of instilling energy or planning some action.

hungry. (1) Eager, avid (*hungry* for affection); (2) strongly motivated (as by ambition).

insane. Absurd, extreme, without consideration and regardless of the facts or beliefs of others.

instructional. The action, practice, or profession of teaching (i.e., *instructional* videos).

intensity. Demonstrating an extreme degree of strength, force, energy, commitment, or feeling.

invest. To involve, commit resources, or engage in some activity or study.

iPod. A brand of portable media player designed and marketed by Apple.

irrational. Not governed by or according to reason; without reason. This is used in the good sense of irrational. (i.e., be *irrational* in the level of actions you are willing to take in order to realize your dreams.)

Jesus Christ. Jesus of Nazareth, the son of Mary; source of the Christian religion.

knock off. The act of not discontinuing some activity.

know. (1) To have understanding of; (2) to have experience and confidence of something; (3) to be aware of the truth or factuality of.

knowledge. Certainty gained through experience, study of or understanding of a science, art, or technique. Information is not knowledge.

Kroc, Ray. (October 5, 1902–January 14, 1984) Took over the (at the time) small-scale McDonald's Corporation franchise in 1954 and built it into the most successful fast food operation in the world.

lack. To be short of something.

lazy. Not inclined to activity or exertion, not energetic or vigorous, usually caused by a lack of purpose.

liability. Person, event, or action that may expose or make others subject to some usually adverse possibility.

lifestyle. The typical way of life of an individual, group, or culture.

literature. The body of writings on a particular subject.

locked up. Unable to shift, fixed in some idea or belief.

logical. (1) Of, relating to, involving, or being in accordance with logic; (2): skilled in logic; (3) formally true or valid, analytic, deductive.

Lombardi, Vince. (June 11, 1913–September 3, 1970) He was the head coach of the Green Bay Packers of the NFL from 1959–1967, winning five league championships during his nine years.

long recession. A period of economic contraction that lasts longer than an average length of a recession which is about 18 months.

magnify. To enlarge in fact or in appearance.

mantra. A commonly repeated word or phrase.

market share. The percentage of the market for a product or service that a company holds or occupies.

marketing campaigns. A connected series of operations designed to promote, sell, and distribute a product or service.

marketplace. A place where there is trade or economic activity—could be a swap meet or an entire economy.

Mary Kay. A brand of skin-care cosmetics and color cosmetics sold by Mary Kay, Inc. Mary Kay World Headquarters is located in Addison, Texas, a Dallas suburb.

misnomer. Something that is incorrect or a false belief.

momentum. The energy that is caused by previous actions.

money. Something generally accepted as a medium of exchange, a measure of value, or a means of payment, like currency.

motives. Something that causes a person to act, react, or respond. The reason someone may take action.

movers and shakers. People that appear to make things happen and get things done.

MLM (multilevel marketing). Also known as network marketing, a marketing strategy that compensates promoters of direct-selling companies not only for product sales they personally generate, but also for the sales of others they introduced to the company.

must. To not have a choice.

myth. An unfounded or false notion, something believed by many but not true.

negativity. (1) Lacking positive qualities; especially disagreeable; (2) marked by features of hostility, withdrawal, or pessimism that hinder or oppose constructive treatment or development; (3) promoting a person or cause by criticizing or attacking the competition.

necessity level. The magnitude of the pressure of circumstance, something that forces an action, a requirement not a choice, urgent need or desire, in relation to something else.

negotiate. To confer with another with the hopes of arriving at a settlement of some matter. (*Note:* While most believe that *negotiate* means to accept a lower price, negotiating has nothing to do with discounting the price of your product or service.)

neurochemistry. The study of the chemical makeup and activities of nerves and the like.

newsletter. A small or large publication containing news of interest chiefly to a special group.

norm. A principle considered to be a right action agreed upon by the members of a group and serving to guide, control, or regulate proper and acceptable behavior. (Just because it is the norm doesn't mean it is correct.)

nurture. To pay attention in order to improve something.

NuSkin. An American direct-selling company that sells cosmetics, nutritional supplements, and technology services. It was founded by Nedra Dee Roney and Blake M. Roney in 1984.

Obama, Barack. Born August 4, 1961, Obama is the 44th and current president of the United States. He is the first African American to hold the office. Obama was the junior United States senator from Illinois.

objection. Considered to be a reason or argument presented in opposition, a feeling or expression of disapproval. (*Note:* Most objections are merely complaints.)

occupancy. The fact or condition of being lived in or filling a space.

offset. Something that counterbalances or compensates for something else (*offset* the pullback).

Oil Crisis. The 1973 oil crisis started on October 15, 1973, when the members of Organization of Arab Petroleum Exporting Countries, or the OAPEC, proclaimed an oil embargo.

old school. Something from the past, not updated. This is not meant that it is wrong, but an older way of thinking that is not current.

oops. Used typically to express a mistake, goof, or dismay.

opportunities. A favorable situation of circumstances that makes for a win, a chance for advancement or progress.

overtly. Out in the open, not hidden, obvious to view, opposite of *covert* or *hidden*.

participate. To take part; be involved as a player not a spectator.

passive. Existing or occurring without being active, open, or direct; not actively participating.

peddle. (1) To sell, promote, or offer something for sale; (2) disseminate.

Peninsula Hotel. An ultra-luxury hotel operator based in Hong Kong. Their flagship hotel is the famous Peninsula Hong Kong.

perceive. To view or sense something.

perfect. To improve or refine or make better than it was, or the idea situation.

pinned down. Unable to move or get up.

playtime. A time for diversion or recreation.

positive. A good effect, favorable, marked by optimism.

power base. (1) The starting point for an action or undertaking where you are in favor and have some control, authority, or influence. (2) Your circle of influence: friends, family, relatives, and current customers.

price sensitive. Showing concern or sensitivity for price as a critical issue or focus.

prima donna. A vain or undisciplined person who operates as an individual and does not typically work well with the team.

problems. Those things, people, or circumstances that are sources of perplexity, distress; opposition to a solution. (*Note:* Problems are opportunities to improve some condition.)

produce. To create through action, intellectual or physical effort; to yield some result or product.

product. Something of value that is marketed, sold, or traded.

product line. Group of products manufactured by a firm that are closely related in use, production, and marketing requirements.

production. The total results of an individual's, company's, or country's efforts.

profit. The amount of returns resulting from the price something is sold for less expenses or cost of that product.

profitable. Endeavors that result in a surplus of positive results that exceed the cost of those efforts.

programmed. Operating based on certain input or beliefs, like a robot or a computer is instilled with data to produce certain answers. Humans can also be programmed.

proposition. (1) An offering for consideration or acceptance; (2) proposal.

prosper. (1) To succeed in an enterprise or activity; (2) *to win or* achieve economic success.

protocol. A way of doing something or a code suggesting strict adherence or way of doing something.

psychological. Relating to the mind and behavior.

psychologists. Those that claim they study the mind and behavior. My personal experience is that these people merely judge and evaluate their clients and further confuse. They have no specific plan for improvement, tend to blame mommy and daddy for everything that is wrong with the client, and a majority of them promote medication for their clients.

psychosomatic. Symptoms caused by the mind.

public office. A position, elected or appointed, that exercises functions for those they are suppose to serve.

PR (public relations). The business of promoting to the public understanding for and goodwill of their person, firm, or institution.

PR campaign. A series of operations designed to bring about an awareness and attention for and goodwill toward a person, firm, or institution.

pullback. Reversal in growth, opposite of *expansion*.

pundit. A person who gives opinions in an authoritative manner, usually through the media.

purpose. A reason for doing something, an object or end to be attained, an intention. (Purpose is the key to motivation.)

qualify. To determine through questions what it is that best suits a client's needs.

quantitities. The amount or numbers of something—often used in plural.

quarter. A three-month period of time.

quest. A pursuit or search for something or outcome.

quit. (1) To cease normal, expected, or necessary action; (2) to admit defeat or to give up.

quitter. (1) One that gives up the pursuit of something or an activity; (2) *especially:* one who gives up too easily; defeatist.

rail. To scold in harsh or strong language.

rant. To talk in a noisy, excited way that continues on and on in a manner that is highly passionate. (See my "You Can't Handle the Truth" video on YouTube for a great example of ranting.)

ravings. Talk with extreme enthusiasm, also to talk irrationally probably because society makes those that are highly enthusiastic wrong.

reactivate. To make active again, reengage, or start again.

reactive. (Not in the good sense.) Occurring as an automatic out-of-control response to a situation. There is also the positive of acting quickly in response to some situation.

reasonable. In accordance with reason (a *reasonable* theory), the opposite of extreme or excessive. The way this is used in this book is *reasonable* is negative.

rebundled. To package an offering of related products or services in order to create more value.

recession. Period of general economic decline, defined usually as a contraction in the GDP for six months (two consecutive quarters) or longer. Marked by high unemployment, stagnant wages, and a fall in retail sales; a recession generally does not last longer than one year and is much milder than a depression.

referral. A person that has been given to you by another as someone that may have interest in your product or service.

relationship. The state of affairs existing between those who have ongoing dealings with one another.

reluctance. (1) Feeling or showing aversion, hesitation, or unwillingness to do something; (2) lack of desire to do something.

repackage. (1) To package again; (2) *specifically:* to put into a more efficient or attractive form.

resistance. An opposing force or condition that takes actions to stop or prevent.

response. A reply to some communication that could be in many forms, verbal, mail, e-mail, chat, even no response could be considered a response.

restrict. (1) To confine within bounds; (2) restrain.

restrictions. Conditions that restrain or limits to what you can do or think you can do.

résumé. A document that contains a summary or listing of relevant job experience and education. (*Note:* Don't ever rely on a résumé without taking the time to meet the person that you want to hire you.)

revenue. Income produced by a given source.

revitalize. To give new life or vigor to something or an activity.

ridicule. Implies a deliberate, often malicious, belittling, or put down.

rocket ride. A positive experience because of actions taken that would be like rapid travel, as if in a rocket.

Rotary Club. An organization of service clubs located all over the world. It is a secular organization open to all persons regardless of race, color, creed, or political preference. There are more than 32,000 clubs and more than 1.2 million members worldwide. Members usually meet weekly for breakfast, lunch, or dinner as an opportunity to organize work on their service goals.

Rules of Success. Educational program developed by Grant Cardone that states basic laws and actions required to create success and is delivered on CD or DVD.

sale. Contract involving transfer of the possession and ownership (title) of a good or property, or the entitlement to a service, in exchange for money or value.

Sanders, Harland. Also known as Colonel Sanders, he was the founder of Kentucky Fried Chicken.

schedule. Timetable for how activities and milestone events or a person's time are sequenced and phased over the allotted period.

Schultz, Howard. Born July 19, 1953, Schultz is an American entrepreneur best known as the chairman and CEO of Starbucks Coffee.

second money. This is related to the money that comes from a second sale.

second sale. This is a sale made after the first sale as an addition to the first purchase. This is not to be confused with the next time you will sell to someone.

selective. (1) The act of being restrictive in choice; (2) discriminating, highly specific in activity.

selling. (1) The action of building value in your product or service with the goal of having someone take ownership of your proposal; (2) a systematic step-by-step process of repetitive and measurable milestones, by which a salesperson relates his or her offering of a product or service. In business, "nothing happens until someone sells something."

sensory. Of or relating to sensation or to the senses.

service (of service). The act of serving is a helpful act, or is useful labor that does not produce immediately a tangible commodity but benefits all parties involved in some way.

shameless. Having no sense of humiliation, remorse, insensible to disgrace. (In this book I talk about being shameless as a positive quality in order to keep moving forward.)

shock. A sudden or violent mental or emotional disturbance;.

shortcut. A method or means of doing something more directly and quickly than, and often not as thoroughly as, ordinary procedure (not a good thing).

skill. (1) The ability to use one's knowledge effectively and readily in execution or performance; (2) a learned power of doing something competently; (3) a developed aptitude or ability.

snob. (1) One who tends to rebuff, avoid, or ignore those regarded as inferior; (2) one who has an offensive air of superiority in matters of knowledge or taste.

social networking. Online communities of people who share interests and/or activities, or who are interested in exploring the interests and activities of others. Most people are just wasting time here and not utilizing the power to increase relationships to improve production.

social norms. A principle of action binding upon the members of a group and serving to guide, control, or regulate proper and what is considered acceptable behavior.

Social Security. Primarily refers to a social insurance program providing social protection, or protection against socially recognized conditions, including poverty, old age, disability, unemployment, and others.

socialized. Refers to the process of learning one's culture and how to live within it (not a good thing as used in the context of this book).

society. A group of humans characterized by patterns of relationships between individuals who share a distinctive culture or institutions and typically beliefs.

soft economy. An economy that is lacking robust strength, stamina, and/or endurance.

solicit. To obtain by usually urgent requests or pleas.

solution. An action or process of solving a problem; solutions always result in an improvement in conditions.

spend. (1) To pay money, usually in exchange for goods or services; (2) to use a resource, such as time.

sphere of influence. Relating to an individual, the area in which because of relationship, authority, or reputation, has the act or power of producing an effect.

stall. To put off, hold off, divert, or delay.

standards. Something set up and established by authority as a rule for the measure of something.

stream. A steady succession (as of words or events); a constantly renewed or steady supply.

success. Results of attaining that which you are moving toward, a favorable or desired outcome; the attainment of wealth, favor, eminence, or some desired outcome.

sufficient. Enough to meet the needs of a situation or a proposed end.

sum total. Total result; totality.

super-freak. An ardent enthusiast to an excessive degree; someone who goes all the way!

supplier. External entity that supplies relatively common, off-the-shelf, or standard goods or services, as opposed to a contractor or subcontractor who commonly adds specialized input to deliverables. Also called a *vendor*.

suppress. (1) To put down by authority or force; (2) subdue, to restrain from a usual course or action; (3) to inhibit the growth or development of.

surrounding agreement. The thinking and ideas of the group or environment around you.

survey. (1) The act of examining as to condition, situation, value, or appraise; (2) act of querying (someone) in order to collect data for the analysis of some aspect of a group or area.

survive. To remain alive or in existence, to live on, to continue to function or prosper. (Most people think of surviving as just getting by, but that is not the definition used here.)

swing for the fences. Baseball jargon suggesting swinging in an effort to hit a home run; in business, it means going for it in a big way.

talking head. A person who talks in front of a video camera.

Ten Commandments. A list of religious and moral imperatives that, according to Judeo-Christian tradition, were authored by God and given to Moses on the mountain referred to as Mount Sinai (Exodus 19:23) or Horeb (Deuteronomy 5:2) in the form of two stone tablets.

ten times. Multiplied results by the number 10.

therein. In that particular respect (i.e., *therein* lies the problem).

Thomas Publishing Company. Thomas Publishing Company, LLC, provides industrial buyers and specifiers with up-to-date product information.

thrive. To grow vigorously, flourish; to gain in wealth or possessions, prosper; to progress toward or realize a goal despite of or because of circumstances.

tight (tight schedule). Characterized by firmness or strictness in control or application or in attention to details.

top dog. A person, group, or thing in a position of authority, especially through victory in a hard-fought competition.

toxin. A poisonous substance that is a specific product of the metabolic activities of a living organism and is usually very unstable.

training. The act, process, or method of one who trains; the skill, knowledge, or experience acquired by one who practices and drills.

unemployment rate. Percentage of the total workforce who are unemployed and are looking for a paid job.

unique. Being without a like or equal, unequaled; distinctively characteristic or different from others in which you might compare.

unwavering. To not vacillate between choices, not fluctuate in opinion, allegiance, or direction.

utilize. To make use of.

value. Relative worth or importance.

value-add. Creation of a competitive advantage by bundling, combining, or packaging features and benefits that result in greater customer acceptance.

value proposition. Mix of goods and services and price and payment terms offered by a firm to its customers.

vein. Referring to finding gold where there are seen traces that will lead to the load.

vendors. Manufacturer, producer, or seller of products or services to a company.

verbalize. Express something in words.

Wachovia Bank. Based in Charlotte, North Carolina, a diversified, wholly owned financial services subsidiary of Wells Fargo. Wachovia Corporation was purchased by Wells Fargo on December 31, 2008, and it ceased to be an independent corporation on that date.

Wal-Mart. An American public corporation that runs a chain of large discount department stores. It is the world's largest public corporation by revenue and it is the largest private employer in the world and the third-largest utility or commercial employer.

warning. The act of giving advice or counsel; act of calling one's attention to or informing.

Washington Mutual. The former owner of Washington Mutual Bank, (which was the United States' largest savings and loan association). On September 25, 2008, the United States Office of Thrift Supervision (OTS) seized Washington Mutual Bank and placed it into the receivership of the Federal Deposit Insurance Corporation.

wealth. Abundance of valuable material possessions or resources.

willing. Inclined to act or respond.

word of mouth. Generated from person to person regarding some experience.

World Trade Center. This is a complex in Lower Manhattan whose seven buildings were destroyed in 2001.

wow. Used to show strong feelings of pleasure or surprise or a way to describe exemplary service.

Xbox. Video game console produced by Microsoft Corporation. It was Microsoft's first gaming console, and it has a service that allows players to compete online.

zombie. The walking dead or a person who resembles one.

Index

Activating/reactivating clients, 28, 37. *See also* Power base
referrals and, 42, 43, 76, 79, 87, 154
versus sales approach, 41, 59–60
Activities, 130, 153
positive thinking and, 167–170
scheduling of, 149, 153
example, 158–159
wasteful activities, 149–150, 156–157
Add-ons. *See* Second sales
Advertising, 26
dependence on, 8, 26, 50, 191
during economic contraction, 50–51, 129–130, 191
marketing and, 129
public relations and, 131
versus utilizing power base, 26
American Medical Association, 164
Attitude. *See also* Positive thinking; Success
being "hungry," 115, 117–118
versus arrogance, 125
definition of, 116–117

being productive versus being paid, 149–150
being "unreasonable," 18, 36, 42, 49–50, 201, 203–205
belief system and, 172
confidence and, 131, 139
creativity and, 116, 140
toward customers, 41–42, 118
expanding customer base and, 74, 123–125, 154
discipline and, 152–153
during business cycles, 166–167
during economic downturn, 84
placebo effect, 164–165
problems and, 132
recording goals and, 169
scheduling of activities and, 149
self-fulfilling prophecy, 164
studies of, 164
success and, 165–166, 172
willingness and, 151
Amway, 25

Cardone Resources

Visit **www.grantcardone.com/resources**
to download these **FREE** resources:

Want to know how to be100 percent?

Learn how to be 100 percent, 100 percent of the time even when things are not going your way and learn how to bring that attitude to every area of your life!

Want to increase your level of action?

In this program you will learn exactly how much action is enough to get you the results you want. Most people come up just short of what is necessary, which will never happen to you again.

Want to learn how to convert the unsold?

One of the most difficult things for sales people is not making the deal. The more unsold we can turn into sales, the more you will sell and the greater your momentum. Learn how to convert the unsold.

Learn more about the price myth.

Your income is determined by how much you can sell and making sure that the offer you are getting is high enough to warrant selling your product. You will learn how to substantiate your price and get it.

Improve the Value-Add Proposition and Increase Sales.

In this program Grant Cardone will show you how to take price objections and turn them into reasons to close the deal by offering value-add propositions that will not just help you get the deal but increase sales!

Visit **www.grantcardone.com/resources**